MELTDOWN

MELTDOWN

MAKING SENSE OF A CULTURE IN CRISIS

MARCUS HONEYSETT

Inter-Varsity Press

INTER-VARSITY PRESS
38 De Montfort Street, Leicester LE1 7GP, England
Email: ivp@ivp-editorial.co.uk
Website: www.ivpbooks.com

First published 2002
Reprinted 2002, 2006

British Library Cataloguing in Publication Data
A catalogue record for this book is available from the British Library.

ISBN-10: 0-85111-492-X
ISBN-13: 978-0-85111-492-7

Set in Garamond
Typeset in Great Britain by Avocet Typeset, Chilton, Aylesbury, Bucks
Printed and bound in Great Britain by Bookmarque Ltd, Croydon, Surrey

Inter-Varsity Press publishes Christian books that are true to the Bible and that communicate the gospel, develop discipleship and strengthen the church for its mission in the world.

Inter-Varsity Press is closely linked with the Universities and Colleges Christian Fellowship, a student movement connecting Christian Unions in universities and colleges throughout Great Britain, and a member movement of the International Fellowship of Evangelical Students.
Website: www.uccf.org.uk

CONTENTS

Foreword 7
Introduction 9

Part 1: Specific Challenges, Specific Theories 19
1. The Disappearance of Authority 21
2. Absolute Truth and Revelation Are Unacceptable 35
3. How Do We Know What Is Important? 50
4. What Does It Mean to Be a Person? 63
5. How Can We Know What Is Real? 78

Part 2: Challenging a Changing Culture 93
6. The Changing Culture and the Postmodern University 95
7. Postmodern Christian Living 1: Postmodern Bible Reading? 112
8. Postmodern Christian Living 2: The Postmodern Church? 131
9. The Immorality of Postmodernism 146
10. TV and Moral Collapse 168
11. Conclusions: Proclaiming the Authentic Jesus 189

Appendix 1: A Glossary of Postmodern Culture 212
Appendix 2: Suggestions for Further Reading 218

Notes 224

Foreword

A couple of years ago, when I perused a draft of this book, my first reaction was, 'How very much I would like my own two children to read this!' One is a university student; the other is in his last year of secondary education. Now that the draft manuscript has become this book, my initial impressions are only confirmed.

Many contemporary essays and books analyse contemporary culture, explain (or explain away) Postmodernism, thunder dire warnings about current trends or coo appreciatively over every new thing (the Athenian spirit did not die in ancient Athens: Acts 17:21). This book stands out for three reasons.

First, while it betrays the author's knowledge of theory, it is far more accessible than most volumes dealing with this subject. It sports an uncommon amount of that least common gift, common sense.

Second, the text is studded with examples from and allusions to the icons of contemporary culture. Not every work informed by theory can drop in references to the

Simpsons, films, plays, books; not every work of this sort provides useful case studies that make Derrida and Foucault come to life.

Above all, Marcus Honeysett understands what goes into making a Christian worldview, and presents his case with straightforward resolve and plain speech that will prove eminently attractive to those for whom 'Jesus is Lord' is more than a slogan.

D. A. Carson
Trinity Evangelical Divinity School,
Deerfield, Illinois

Introduction

Our culture is the air we breathe. It is the sum of all the events, experiences, influences and communication that we participate in, along with the meaning and value that we attach to them. We are all involved in culture. We may love some parts of it and loathe others but we cannot escape being part of it. We all produce, consume and recycle culture.

Culture is a hot topic among those at the cutting edge of social trends. There is a lot of heated discussion about what culture is, and even more about what defines *valuable* culture. Should something be held to be valuable simply because it is popular? Is *The Simpsons* the high point of our culture because of its widespread appeal in the industrialized West? Or should value be ascribed not to popularity but according to scarcity? Is a Rembrandt a more valuable item simply because it is unique, copyable but unrepeatable? These are big questions not just among philosophers and academics but in the media and politics, among marketeers and students, between artists and architects.

The answers that we give to these questions shape the world that we produce around us. Our decisions are dictated by the things we deem valuable. Significant aspects of our lives, our relationships, our work patterns and our *thinking* are created and moulded by others, whose work is to make us believe that certain things are valuable, but whose vision and ideals may be very different to ours. The TV producer whose editorial policy denies Christians access to the airways but gives significant air time to pro-abortion science. The presenter who whips up a studio audience to enthusiasm over immorality whilst dismissing virtue as 'poor television'. The politician who makes value decisions about what members of her party may discuss in public, suppressing their own private beliefs for party ideals. The academic who teaches tomorrow's movers and shakers that the future can, and *should*, be exactly what they want it to be. The journalist who adds subtle editorial spin to the interview between the clergyman and the gay-rights activist. The president who lies to cover up sexual scandal and is applauded for self-preservation. The list is endless.

Some people have a greater impact on culture than others. Some are able to deliberately manufacture cultural trends. A classic case in point is the recent British TV show *Popstars* in which young hopefuls were auditioned over several weeks to join a new band. So great was the hype that, once formed, the band went straight to number one in the charts despite being totally artificial. The Spice Girls similarly sold twenty million albums on the back of media image-making before they performed a single live concert.

There are powerful cultural forces bidding for our hearts and minds. All of us participate in the outcome. This book is concerned with our culture and how we should live in it as discerning Christians. Its central theme is that some of the most powerful influences of our age are almost invisible, yet are acutely anti-Christian, anti-truth and anti-God. Much of what is taught in universities, for example, is a closed book to most of us, and yet profoundly influences the next generation of decision makers. It may alarm you to discover that some of the most widely taught academic theory today revolves around the suggestion that it is impossible to know things with certainty or to communicate reliably. Woe betide the Christian who stands up in most universities today to affirm that God speaks in the Bible.

What universities and the media teach today, we all have to live with tomorrow. The students go on to write newspapers and produce soap operas. Scientific research done on the basis of theory that would raise the eyebrows of many cannot be undone. Whatever our thoughts may be about genetic modification, for example, the genie is now out of the bottle and there is no going back.

This book is written for any thoughtful Christian who wants to examine how the world is being shaped around us. It asks how we should respond Christianly to today's world. Many in the media, in politics and in the universities are deliberately trying to 'think the future'. Unless Christians are careful cultural observers and critics, we shall certainly be more shaped by our environment than responsible for shaping it. This book began life as a survey among Christian undergraduate students in the UK. It asked about the sort of things they were being taught and the *way* in which they were being taught. Many of the answers given would come as no surprise to anyone who has ever read anything on Postmodernism. The more alarming factor was the frequency with which students said that they were forced to regurgitate highly corrosive theory as fact, while removing their own, often coherent and well reasoned, arguments in order to gain academic acceptability. In some cases this amounted to little more than brutal suppression of anyone who had the courage to admit to believing in truth.

Defining Postmodernism

Much has been written in recent years on what has become known as *Postmodernism.* 'Postmodernism' is a notoriously slippery word to define but at its heart lie three key concepts. The first is *relativism* – the idea that all claims about truth are only relative to other claims. For the Postmodernist there is no absolute truth and no God to define what truth is. The second central concept is that of *philosophical pluralism* – the idea that, because truth is relative, all ideas and truth claims must be treated with equal respect, there being no objective way to evaluate their respective merits. The third big idea of Postmodernism is a suspicion of anything that claims to be true or to have all the answers. Jean Francois Lyotard, a famous French philosopher, referred to this as a suspicion of 'metanarratives' – large-scale stories that claim to be true. Christianity is immediately suspect because it claims to be true for everyone.

The results of these concepts are evident throughout everyday life. The ideas are there for all to see; in books and films, in popular music, and on the internet. Politicians are so frightened of the resulting political correctness that they shy away from positive policies into negative campaigning. TV moguls produce completely artificial entertainment shows and successfully market them as truthful 'reality TV'. Worse still are the shows that air personal problems for the consumption of studio audiences with no thought for truth or morality. Jerry Springer's show often seems little more than the modern equivalent of the circus freak show. Truth and morality don't usually make for entertaining TV, it is believed. And, of course, slumping church attendance is closely linked to a general lack of confidence in the message of the gospel in society at large and, sadly, among many Christians.

Postmodern corrosion

Corrosive forces are powerfully at work in the world today. At the heart of Postmodernism, and therefore at the heart of much of contemporary culture, is a denial of God, of sin, of truth and a corresponding enthroning of self. In universities it is the most provocative theory that attracts funding. In the popular media there is no criticism of films like *Pulp Fiction*, that celebrate violence, or *Four Weddings and a Funeral*, with its joyful acceptance of unfaithfulness. Indeed they are warmly received. In the music world a so-called artist like Eminem is acclaimed despite lyrics which defend rape, torture and the abuse of women.

Most people accept the underlying assumptions behind all these phenomena unthinkingly because we fail to view the world through Christian spectacles. We miss the fact that culture is not neutral but contains a large number of messages and agendas in which we are invited to participate. Our culture is in a state of meltdown because we have disposed of truth in order to live without God. No wonder that the media so readily celebrate complete freedom from moral restraint. At an academic level people have been saying for years that morality is outdated and the new generation simply takes this for granted. And yet the sense of spiritual lostness is acute. While people have junked truth, we cannot similarly dispose of yearning for God. He has put eternity in the hearts of men and women, and no matter how much we would like to suppress this fact, it won't go away. Interest in 'spirituality', defined in a vague and mystical way, is at an all-time high. Modernism promised heaven on earth through scientific progress. It told us that we simply didn't need redeeming and saving because we could do it all ourselves. It triumphantly proclaimed the death of God and the self-sufficiency of humanity. Modernism had no place for spirituality and steadfastly maintained that we just don't need it. Modernism was wrong.

The challenge to the gospel

In its place Postmodernism has produced a huge spirituality industry designed to pamper every individual's sense of personal need for fulfilment. For the demise of Modernism has not sent hungry people back to the gospel and to truth. The influx of Eastern religion into post-Christian societies simply reflects Postmodernism's suspicion of truth. Verifiable truth, evidence, and whether or not events such as the crucifixion and resurrection of Christ actually happened, are marginal concerns for the Buddhist or the New Ager. In Postmodern religion it doesn't matter whether God has spoken in order to reveal himself reliably. And so the new interest in religion is just as bankrupt as the old disinterest.

The new interest is, however, more subtle and dangerous. In a previous generation the opponents of Christianity were outspoken in their challenge and forthright in their assault. In this generation the opponents of Christianity have a veneer of tolerant acceptance. We often hear that it is fine to be a Christian as long as we don't try to convert anyone. For that would be to claim that Christianity is true for all. And more often still we meet people who have a syncretistic blend of ideas, some Christian, others far from Christian, yet believing themselves to be Christian. A film like *The Matrix* is a good example, with a myriad of themes so clearly recognizable by Christians that it is easy to think it is a Christian film, despite the Buddhist martial-arts influences and the clearly Postmodern/mystical theory that the world is all illusory. If you watch carefully, one key Postmodern writer actually appears in the movie! Sadly, today we also discover corroded churches that have lost the gospel, kowtowing to the pressure of the world to settle into a ghetto and live the quiet life.

The pressure to conform

Pressure comes in two shades. Firstly there is peer pressure to conform. The world hates nobody as much as the person who refuses to conform and Postmodernism delights in trying to reduce everything to the lowest common denominator of 'tolerance'. Often, however, the only thing that is not tolerated is genuine, loving, outspoken Christianity, for Jesus Christ makes universal claims on the obedience and submission of all. The second shade is the outright assault that occurs when Christians refuse to toe the line.

Surviving pressure is hard. It is made all the harder when we don't recognize or understand the subtle influences to which we are subjected. Most of us are not experts on culture. This book was originally intended to be a kind of survival guide to help with the crucial job of understanding our culture and trying to think Christianly about it. I hope that it will provide sufficient background in contemporary theories to help the reader understand the challenges and see the points of disagreement between the gospel and contemporary thought. I hope too that the book may begin to suggest ways to be confident in the gospel and how to use the gospel to disarm twenty-first-century secularism.

Christian responses to Postmodernism tend to fall into one of two categories. Either they are highly academic and likely to appeal little to the average Christian reader, or they can be highly populist but fail to engage at any depth with the most important non-Christian writers who are usually extremely difficult to understand. In this book I have tried to tread a middle path.

Part 1 takes five key essays from cutting-edge secular theorists and examines them from a Christian viewpoint. The essays discussed are often difficult but profoundly influential. I have done my best to explain their main points simply. You must be the judge of whether I have succeeded. Each of these five chapters also contains a case study and questions to help the reader think about how we might meet the theory in everyday life. In each chapter there are also suggested Christian responses to the essays and ideas about how to be more confident in the gospel when facing a hostile and anti-Christian world.

Part 2 further examines the influences that have brought our culture to its current state and asks about the moral consequences of Postmodernism and how it seeps into our lives and into the church of Jesus Christ. As we have said, culture is the air we breathe. If we breathe a corrosive atmosphere, then it will eat away at our inner convictions, attitudes and values. It will change the things we believe and our attitude to being members of Christ's church. Alongside a careful understanding of our culture, it is vital that we examine ourselves and our churches in order to diagnose whether we are being authentically biblical Christians or whether we have already been swept off course by the tide of contemporary culture.

How to read this book

Meltdown started life as a study guide. Study questions have been retained in each chapter. They are not essential to make sense of the book but taking time to pause and answer them will help the reader get to grips with the more difficult and abstract parts of contemporary culture. It will also aid in evaluating which battles are worth fighting and which are not. We surely need to be open enough to ideas that we can engage meaningfully with our culture without being *needlessly* critical, and yet firm enough on the gospel that we do not shift our ground on questions of key importance. Only if we walk this tightrope will we avoid the twin dangers of apostasy on the one hand and unthinking and ugly polemic on the other. The book is also written to allow the reader either to dip into the specific subjects dealt with in Part 1 or to work through the book consecutively. If you choose not to read the whole of Part 1, I hope you will still find Part 2 accessible and helpful.

Many people have had a hand in the shaping of this book. Special thanks go to Professor Don Carson for kindly agreeing to write the Foreword, Colin Duriez at IVP, and also to Helen Campbell, Sam Chaplin, Marilyn and Kathryn Coles, Liz Capper, Norman Fraser, Andy Shudall and especially to my wife Ros who has suffered enough seminars on Postmodernism to last her a lifetime.

Part 1

Specific Challenges, Specific Theories

The catch-all term *Postmodernism* is a haven for a whole variety of ideas and theories. Together these ideas form a powerful bastion of our prevailing culture of anti-truth. (See Chapter 6 for a short explanation of how things got this way.) Many contemporary books, plays and films and much of the fashion, design, journalism and teaching of recent times reflect the culture of anti-truth. These products of our culture often deliberately reflect deeply un-Christian or post-Christian values and ideas.

To make an impact on our culture we cannot afford to deal purely with the theory or purely with the cultural products that go with it. We must do both. Part 1 addresses five specific ideas or theories that challenge Christians in the area of truth. These and their key exponents are: the disappearance of authority (Michel Foucault); deconstruction (Jacques Derrida); the question of value (Walter Benjamin); identity and sexuality (Judith Butler); and the disappearance of reality (Jean Baudrillard).

These five, out of many possibilities, have been chosen for two reasons. They are key areas of theory that in turn are influential over other theories and ideas, and the people behind them are some of the biggest names in contemporary culture. We should not ignore the fact that style is extremely important in Postmodern theory, and therefore the theorist can be almost as important as the theory. The most outlandish ideas are given a veneer of avant-garde excitement if they come from a Derrida or a Baudrillard.

All five areas have their roots in relativism and pluralism. It is worth refreshing our memories about these terms.

Relativism is the idea that things, ideas and claims to truth only relate to each other, not to anything external. There is nothing objective by which to measure truth claims. Hence no statement about truth can transcend the culture within which it is made. *No truth claim can have overarching significance for all.* Of course, we only have to define culture narrowly enough, and we reach the conclusion that nobody can speak truth that is relevant to anyone else at all – you have your truth, I have mine.

Pluralism comes in two flavours. Empirical pluralism – the fact that we live in a multifaceted culture – is neither positive nor negative. It just is. Philosophical pluralism, on the other hand, is definitely negative. Based on relativistic assumptions, this is the idea that we cannot speak truth that is relevant to others. All claims to truth are equally valid and there is no way to judge or evaluate between them.

Each of the five chapters in Part 1 takes a piece of contemporary theory, usually a short essay, and examines the argument put forward in the light of a case study. I try to suggest the beginnings of a Christian response. Copyright reasons don't allow us to print the essays here. None of them are easy to read but the essays by Foucault and Benjamin are perhaps more accessible than the others, if you want a taster of the way that contemporary philosophers write. I recommend that you try to answer the questions in each chapter as you go along.

Chapter 1
The Disappearance of Authority

Case study

Mike is a media professional in your church. Recently he has started to gain public recognition for producing a variety of historical programmes on television. Until recently, however, he hasn't really thought much about whether being a Christian should make any difference to the way he reports history.

First a newspaper article accused him of being politically incorrect after the broadcasting of a programme he made on the British Raj in India.

'They called me an imperialist propagandist,' he tells you indignantly after a Sunday service. 'I know as well as anyone else that colonialism was far from a good deal for all, but I wanted to show that there were some positive points too. It seems that some people don't want to hear that.'

Then Mike was invited to participate in a public debate on 'Real History – Can We Ever Know What Happened?' Mike took a pounding that day in a packed debating chamber.

'It felt like absolutely nobody there thought that you can say

meaningful or true things about history,' Mike says. 'I had heard that the latest trendy thinking teaches that we have to treat historical texts with caution, but I didn't think it would be as vicious as this. I'm just a TV producer. Granted, a programme has to have an angle – but I do want the facts behind the angle first. These people didn't seem to think much about facts. In fact the chair of the debate finished by publicly questioning whether we can know anything reliable about historical figures. Or contemporary ones, for that matter.'

In the following week Mike does a little research, which he later shares with you.

'It seems that what people are teaching and the papers are picking up on is the fact that truth is held under great suspicion,' he says. 'In the case of historical documents, people have always said that history is written by the winners, but now people laugh at any idea of communicating truthfully. And at the idea of anyone having the authority to speak truthfully. They are saying that truth is oppressive and that we can't know anything. It sounds crazy, but I am starting to get quite worried about it.'

'Why would this worry you?'

'Well, if people are saying we can't communicate truthfully, doesn't that ultimately mean that we can't know things? That we can't have any confidence that the things we say are accurate or the things we believe are true? That worries me deeply. I know TV gets a bad press, but some of us really do want truthful, honest, valuable broadcasting. This stuff would seem to make a mockery of things we think are important.'

You ask Mike how he thinks he should react as a Christian to these kinds of ideas.

'Somebody asked me that in the debate,' he says. 'They thought that knowing facts depends on being there – you know, being aware of the context something is said or done in. They said that because we are not there we can't know anything. We can't know what a writer meant. We can't know

who was doing right or wrong. And then they challenged me as a Christian, telling me that I don't have a time-machine to know first-hand about Bible stories, let alone the ability to second-guess a dead author. I didn't really know what to say. What would you have said?'

Mike is determined to think out what Christians should believe about ideas like this. He realizes that if God cannot communicate in the Bible and nobody else can communicate at all, then it makes it very difficult to trust God and to know him. And it makes it impossible to believe that the Bible has authority over us as we try to obey what God has said.

'And that way,' he reflects, 'lies spiritual shipwreck, surely?'

Some questions

What would you say to Mike? Pause and consider these questions:

1. Describe the issues with which Mike is wrestling.
2. What underlying assumptions from relativism and pluralism do they contain?
3. What sort of effect might each assumption have on Mike's life, witness and work as a TV producer?
4. How would you help him to think them through?

The theory bit: *Michel Foucault*

Ideas like these, which challenge the possibility of truthfulness and reliable knowledge, are big currency in our society. Many people are taught them at university. Mike needn't be a media professional; the ideas are just as important in a whole range of subjects and careers. Underlying Mike's concerns is the fundamental concept that it is not possible to know someone through their writing or speaking, in such a way that they may have authority over us.

A key writer in this area is Michel Foucault (pronounced Foo-ko). He starts a famous essay 'What Is An Author?'

with the theme: 'What does it matter who is speaking?' He concludes that it doesn't matter – that authors are unknowable and not authoritative. Foucault's ideas are closely linked to the thoughts of the philosopher Friedrich Nietzsche about the unknowableness of God. Nietzsche roundly proclaimed that 'God is dead.' Foucault's ideas about authority follow on from what happens if you believe in a world without God. Here is a summary of Foucault's train of thought in 'What Is An Author?'

Foucault maintains that the idea of an Author, who communicates clear and obvious meaning in their work, is a modern idea. Nobody thought this way until recently, he says. Basically it is all about money and copyright. Authorship seems to make the individual more important than the group or the community. It is, Foucault says, an attractive idea.

He goes on to say, however, that actual authors aren't knowable. Therefore facts about them do not really matter. Who really cares where Shakespeare lived, or whether Augustine borrowed material from other people? Foucault says that the *works* of an author, the books, plays, films they make, are the only ways we have through which we can know them. Therefore what they *wanted* to communicate is not really important, because we cannot tell whether they really wanted to say a particular thing or not. Foucault says that the author's intentions are something we just can't get at. Hence he concludes that the real joy of a text is not in its content, but in the ways we can play with it, use it for our own ends and enjoy it in our own ways.

From this move away from an interest in the content of the text it follows that we cannot really talk about an author being authoritative over a work or body of work. They don't control their works once they are in the public domain. They can't dictate anything about them, most of all about what they mean. And who should say what an authoritative body of work should contain? If we found Shakespeare's laundry lists, should we put them on a par with *Hamlet*? In UK schools it is not unknown to find Shakespeare replaced with contemporary thrillers. Why? Because people believe that the important and valuable work is not the one that has lasted over the centuries, or the technically sophisticated one, but the one that the individual enjoys most. The way the text is received is seen to be what gives it value. The reader is king.

Foucault's next step is to say that, because we can't know an author's intentions, they become hidden figures. Their writing always needs interpreting. But the rub is that, because we are unable to know the context they wrote in, interpretation of original meaning is not possible. Therefore Foucault begins his essay: 'What does it matter who is speaking?' Of course, it doesn't!

If all we can know about an author is their text, then the author has lost the authority to communicate their meaning through the text. Interpretation is more important to Foucault than communication. And as we cannot know original meaning, and nobody can offer interpretations of the text that are self-evidently true or valid for all, what matters is not what the author wants to say, but how every single individual wishes to interpret the text. In other words, I can make a text mean what I want it to mean.

It follows that the name or character of an author no longer guarantees the value or truth of a document. For Foucault the only one who can give meaning or value to a text is the reader – and it is quite all right to bring your own meaning. Any implication of truth or original meaning being accessible through reading is dismissed.

Hence a good piece of writing is not seen as one that communicates really valuable things or important truths. Instead it is one we can use for our own ends.

Foucault therefore insists that we cannot know the

author of a text, nor trust their authoritative value judgments or truth claims. And then he takes a final step by saying that it isn't just literature that is a text, but painting, music and other arts. More recently philosophers have taken to defining the whole world as a text, and using Foucault's arguments to deny any meaning at all in the world apart from ones that seem right for the individual.

A summary of Foucault's argument

We could summarize Foucault's argument like this:

1. Authorship is a modern idea.
2. We cannot know an author.
3. Therefore the author does not have authority.
4. Hence we need to interpret.
5. We cannot interpret the original author – so we can all bring our own interpretations.
6. I can bring any meaning I like. I can use the text however I like.
7. Everything in the world is a text – I can understand anything in the world however I like.

Some questions

1. Is any of Foucault's theory relevant to Mike's situation?
2. Is Foucault right or wrong? Why?
3. What are the flaws in the argument? Is there anything you can affirm in the argument?
4. How does Foucault's argument relate to the way we understand Scripture?

A Christian response to Foucault

Truth

As Christians we believe in truth. We believe that God exists, that he created everything and knows everything about his creation. We believe that God has spoken through many means, most crucially in the person of God the Son, Jesus Christ, and through the witness to him that we find in the Bible. Christians believe, on good evidence, that the Bible is true and accurate and that the Holy Spirit still speaks today through the Word that he inspired the biblical writers to write. In short, we believe that we can know things truly because God speaks intelligibly. We also believe we can act on the truth in order to live God's way in God's world.

If Foucault is right, all these things are jeopardized. His argument is the end of all meaning and all significance. If it is correct, then we can never know whether anything is truthful or not and we can never distinguish right from wrong. Foucault firmly held that it is not possible to know truth at all and therefore that he had licence to behave exactly as he wished with no recriminations. And he did behave this way – though there were recriminations aplenty. He was a professor at a University in California, lived an outrageously gay lifestyle and finally died of AIDS. It would not be too strong to say that the ideas Foucault taught created the conditions that killed him, by promoting unbridled immorality. He had the courage of his convictions and those convictions were his undoing, because they governed his behaviour (see Chapter 9).

Before we examine Foucault's argument I want to make this key point: that immoral theory creates the conditions for immoral living. If we believe wrongly then we will act wrongly. In all the chapters that follow, the contemporary ideas we discuss have profound implications for our moral understanding of ourselves and how we should live. We need to think and read prayerfully in order to see how, in contrast, we should live to please, not ourselves, but our God who made us for himself.

Foucault's argument

The first four points in Foucault's argument, as outlined above, are all about interpretation. Interpretation should be the process by which we discover what the original author of a text meant to communicate to the original readers. In biblical interpretation the first question we should always ask is 'What did it mean to its original hearers?' Only then can we ask what it means for us today.

Foucault, however, says that the original author and the original readers are unknowable. Hence the process of interpretation is impossible. There is no certain core of meaning to discover. All we have is the text in itself, without any controls on the way we should use it. We can treat it however we like and make it mean whatever we like. The attraction of this argument, as with much relativist theory, is that it is true up to a point. With most texts there is a limit to what we can know about the author, their circumstances and their thought processes. We will never fully appreciate every nuance, idiom and metaphor. Foucault rightly warns us to beware of dogmatism in interpretation. However, to say that texts are not open to interpretation is an unnecessary step for several reasons.

The first reason is that our inability to know a *whole* context does not mean that we cannot truly know *some* context. There is a misunderstanding here between knowing something correctly and knowing something exhaustively. Evidence may well lead to a correct conclusion, even if that conclusion is not a hundred per cent scientifically proveable.

Secondly, the fact that we cannot know *everything* an author intended to communicate does not mean we cannot know *anything*. This is to question the whole nature of communication. We do communicate successfully all the time, and translate with a degree of success between our own language and a variety of other languages and sign systems (e.g. road signs).

Thirdly, the fact that we cannot fully interpret *every* nuance of a text does not mean that we cannot move in the right direction in our interpretation. Our interpretation can become more accurate as we work at it, and we can know we are on the right track because the meaning fits better with what we do know of the context. Humility is obviously needed here – none of us is infallible. But as Don Carson helpfully points out, like the curve in mathematics that approaches a line more and more closely but never actually reaches it, so our interpretation will never be perfect, but it can be very nearly perfect.

A fourth reason that counts against the impossibility of interpretation of texts is this: the fact that we do not have *all* circumstances in common with the author does not mean that we do not have *any* in common. The more radical edge of contemporary theory concludes that we literally have nothing in common with each other – that we do not belong to the same *humanity* as each other. As Christians we know that we are all made in God's image and that the Holy Spirit helps us to read and understand the Bible. In other words, the author is not absent and unknowable, but right there alongside us as we read what he wrote!

A fifth reason is Foucault's questionable assumption that without the presence of the author the text itself contains no help on how to interpret it. We do need to be careful when deciding exactly what sort of writing we are interpreting, what genre of literature it is. We will misinterpret if, for example, we approach a poem as a letter or a book of prophecy as an allegorical story, or a gospel as a novel. Much contemporary writing is deliberately and difficultly ironic in order to try to confound interpretation. But to deny that any writing can be straightforward is, once again, an unnecessary step. It assumes that *all* writers are trying to deceive by writing code to which they provide no codebook.

The greatest flaw in Foucault's theory is that he assumes that because meaning and interpretation are always open to *some* question, it is therefore impossible to communicate *any* meaning faithfully. It is a false conclusion arrived at by pushing a position to an illogical extreme.

The uniqueness of Scripture

Not only do Chistians believe in truth. We also are committed to the uniqueness of Scripture. We therefore need to distinguish carefully between the Bible and any other text. However great the creativity of a human author, and however plain the message that they communicate, they are still fallen people in a fallen world. To some extent the author *must* fail to be a perfect communicator, just as their text will always fail to be perfect, and just as a reader will always fail to interpret perfectly.

Scripture, however, has its foundations in the unchangeable character of God. He knows everything perfectly and reveals himself and his purposes perfectly. His Spirit still controls interpretation. While people come to a variety of conclusions about exactly how God used the human authors of the Bible to write his words, the overriding fact remains that God is the author of Scripture. And this author is not dead, but living.

Christians and interpretation

Christians believe that even though we are fallen and quite capable of misunderstanding, we not only have accurate access to the text, but also to the author and interpreter of the text. We in fact have a family relationship with that author. Furthermore, we know our lives to be transformed in Christ-likeness when we obey what the Bible really says. This pragmatic transforming power demonstrates right understanding. We know and trust the God who reveals himself. We are happy to accept what he reveals, and leave what he doesn't to him. We also know that a scriptural world-view is coherent. It describes the world we know. This world-view has changed and still changes people's lives.

Any understanding of the world, or 'world-view', aspires to *correspond* to reality (i.e. to describe the world as it really is), to be *coherent* within itself (i.e. to be consistent), and to have *transforming power* (i.e. to actually work when we put it into practice). Anything claiming to be a true world-view must satisfy not one, but all three of these criteria. Christians believe that the Bible reveals God and his purposes as they really are. We believe that the Bible describes the world accurately. For this reason we must be ready, even eager, to subject our world-view to scrutiny. If the Bible is true, if we really can interpret correctly as the Holy Spirit helps us, then we will discover that our understanding of God, the world and ourselves is closely in tune with reality. In addition, we should expect that knowing, obeying and loving God should satisfy the third test – that our characters should be changing and becoming more like Jesus.

In contrast to this Christian world-view and understanding of the text of the Bible, Foucault says that the process of communication contains three elements: the author, the text and the reader. Foucault claims that the first two of these are flawed and uncertain and that control over the meaning of the text therefore rests with the reader (so-called 'reader response' theory). In response, therefore, Christians must work hard to show that, for Scripture at least, it is the first two that are absolute and guaranteed, while the third may be flawed. Reader response theory is an attractive position for sinful people, but not a humble one. And for all non-biblical texts we can say that communication (while fallen and conditioned by Babel) is still God-given and is enabled by the humanity we share. Even a cursory glance at our everyday lives tells us that we communicate accurately all the time, even translating foreign languages and signs. It is not unusual for friends to be able to complete sentences for one another. These things point not to an explosion of meaning and an inability to communicate, but to a common God-given humanity. There are right ways to understand the world and wrong ones.

When we apply ourselves to the pursuit of truth, then having a correct moral outlook limits our interpretations in correct ways. There is an intimate link between interpretation and morality. On the one hand, if we believe correctly, and are determined to obey God, then we will live correctly. On the other hand, as we are determined to live correctly under his rule, then we can expect his help in understanding correctly. It is no mistake that the Bible so often says that the fear of the Lord is the beginning of wisdom.

Authority

Not only do Christians believe in truth, and the uniqueness of Scripture, but also in the authority of the author of Scripture. Therefore, far from value judgment being completely relative and depending on the reader in all cases, Christians hold that authoritative decisions about meaning lie with the author – in the case of the Bible, God. When we believe his Word and trust him, this makes a difference in the real world.

Foucault's definition of a good piece of writing is false. It is not a text with which you can do your own thing, or one for which the only important thing is our opinions. We were created by the God who reveals himself truly. The things that ultimately matter in this universe are his purposes and not ours. Absolute meaning cannot be known or acted on with total confidence from merely human authorship, but it can be known and trusted if it is revealed from above.

Jesus said that the only person who can speak truly of eternal things, of ultimate realities, is the One who has come from heaven (John 3:12). He tells us not only that his words are therefore reliable, but that if we believe and trust him that we will experience his totally transforming power: we are born again from heaven and receive eternal life!

How does this affect our church member Mike?

Mike is being bombarded with the idea that, because we cannot know absolutely everything, therefore we can know nothing. Thus he is meeting many who are open to rewriting history. This rewriting is designed not to reveal truth but to empower groups who previously felt they had a rough deal from history. There may be *some* occasional merit in such rewriting, but much is written purely because everything seems up for grabs and some capital might as well be made from the situation. Hence Mike's desire to say anything positive about a colonial institution will produce a huge backlash. Christians often find the same backlash from people who say that missions in the last two centuries and today are nothing more than imperialism.

Mike needs help to stand for truth when his ideas and his integrity are being rubbished. His contemporaries are telling him that claims to truth are only power games or personal preferences. Mike needs to understand that it is not truth that is oppressive. Mere opinion, however, is certainly oppressive when it falsely claims an absolute-truth status for itself. This is frequently true in the media and news reporting where a sound-bite culture often means presenting an editorial side to a story and omitting any conflicting information. The same is true in universities where many students simply capitulate, regurgitating their lecturers' notes in return for acceptance and good marks. Truth is often vilified as oppressive simply because it stands as a constant challenge to human-centred self-actualization.

Mike needs to have confidence that he can really know things from history. Those around him have swallowed the idea that doubts about context and communication can never be answered. They believe that 'what actually happened' is unobtainable and that no question of fact can ever be resolved. He needs help to think through issues of interpretation, how to distinguish between evidence and proof, and the difference between knowing truly and knowing exhaustively.

Mike might value help to make sure that assaults on him in his work environment do not affect his spiritual life. He is doing a good job of relating his faith to his work. He is in an excellent position to engage with issues of knowledge, meaning and interpretation.

Professionally it might be helpful for Mike to get to grips with understanding Foucault's agenda and where it leads, learning about how to do good interpretation and applying it to his work.

Mike can have a wonderful witness in a tough environment. This requires support, encouragement and firm Christian friendship. A person like Mike has many opportunities to shine as a Christian in a field where many have turned their back completely on God.

Chapter 2

Absolute Truth and Revelation Are Unacceptable

The challenge from Jacques Derrida

In the last chapter we discussed the challenge that Michel Foucault raises to meaning and interpretation. If an author cannot communicate meaning, then we can no longer speak of anyone or anything having authority. Nobody can rightly communicate intention, and the very acts of communicating and interpreting are themselves viewed with suspicion. With the challenge to meaning comes a challenge to any truth claim and any authority.

The rejection of authority and truth, and the resulting moral slide, are much wider than just literature. How have the ideas been passed on to other areas of life and thought?

You have probably come across the term 'deconstruction'. It is quite a trendy in-phrase. Deconstruction is the key tool by which the suspicion of texts becomes suspicion of just about anything at all. Deconstruction is a tricky thing to get our minds around. However, it is so vital to every part of culture today that we must try.

Case study

Diane is a leader in the university Christian Union near your church. She studies classics – ancient Greek and Latin. For her final dissertation she has been strongly encouraged to write on ancient texts but with reference to the work of a man called Jacques Derrida, especially his theory of 'deconstruction'. One day you find her in a stressed frame of mind. You ask what the problem is.

She tells you that she is struggling with two things. The first is that she doesn't understand even the first paragraph of the book she has been given on Derrida, but the second and more important struggle is that everything she has heard about Derrida leads her to believe that his theories are difficult for a Christian to accept.

You ask what she has heard.

'Derrida is all the rage in the university Classics department. Obviously, there are no new texts in Classics to bring extra interest to the study. So all the tutors are reading and teaching brand-new theory which tells us to take ancient writings and see how we can use them for our own ends today.'

'Why is that wrong?' you ask.

'Well, I don't know if it is right to just say a writing means anything I want it to mean, for one thing,' Diane replies. 'I mean, what about what the writer originally thought? Doesn't that count for anything? But I am also worried about the sorts of things people seem to use this new theory to support.'

'Such as?'

'Like taking a famous Greek play – Oedipus *maybe – and saying that it whole-heartedly supports current gay rights. Or the idea that because we are not completely in the culture of a dead writer, we cannot understand anything written by them. Or anyone else, for that matter. They say that deconstruction*

teaches that all texts contradict themselves, so there is no real meaning.'

'What effect does that actually have on the Classics department?' you ask.

'All sorts of things. A lot of new staff are recruited because of their interest in feminist or lesbian studies. They really have a go at some of the male students. Sometimes we have practical exercises. One last week involved men dressing as women for a Greek play. There was lots of gay joking and horseplay and the staff encouraged it. But I think the thing that disturbs me most is that nobody listens when anyone tries to express any concern about these things. It seems that they are just excluded from the in-crowd. But the in-crowd just seems to get more and more outrageous and immoral every day. I am not sure I want to be in with that bunch.'

'Why should you be?'

'Well, they get all the best results. They are in the lecturers' pockets. All the stuff that seems to be the most cutting-edge is taught out of hours in seminars that are by invitation only. I'm worried that if I don't go with the crowd I will get a poorer degree, but if I do, it might be very hard to stand up as a Christian. Especially when I don't really understand what is being taught. How can I know whether it is good or bad?'

Some questions

How would you respond to Diane? Consider these questions:

1. What are some of the issues that Diane is struggling with?
2. What underlying assumptions do you detect in the sort of things being taught by the Classics department?
3. How would you try to help Diane understand the issues?

4. What help does Diane need to live as a Christian in the Classics department?

The theory bit: *Jacques Derrida*

Sadly, this case study is not fictitious. It is a combination of conversations I have recently had with a couple of students. We could go to nearly any university department in the Western world, be it English or Geography, Latin or Physics, to find their own outworking of Postmodern theories, among which *deconstruction* is one of the most influential.

It is time to try and define deconstruction. This theory was invented by Jacques Derrida (pronounced Dare-idder), a literary theorist and philosopher. His influence on twentieth-century philosophy is huge. Derrida says that we need new ways of living without absolutes. Deconstruction is his biggest contribution. Before we examine deconstruction, we should try to understand why Derrida calls for such a departure from ideas of absolute truth.

Where is Derrida coming from?

Derrida lays out his stall, among other places, in a hard but very important essay called 'Structure, Sign and Play in the Discourse of the Human Sciences'. You can tell what it is going to be like from the title! His argument goes like this.

Western thought and language have always believed in absolute truth. But if some things are absolutely true then other things are false. This, Derrida claims, unfairly limits what it is possible to think or believe. By providing certainties and making some things taboo, people lose the right to explore anything outside those certainties.

However, Derrida's underlying assumption (which this essay does not explore) is that there is no God in the equation to guarantee such absolutes. Hence ideas about certainty are now what he calls 'ruptured'. He concludes that any idea of a fixed centre for all learning and knowledge is only imposed on us by our past or by institutions of society, and does not in reality exist at all. It is a means by which someone exercises power over us. Hence for Derrida there is no ultimate reality. There is no God outside the system to whom everyone and everything relates. Instead the only relationships that we can know are within the system of the world. Derrida calls these relationships 'discourses'. For him ultimate reality is only a series of these discourses. There is nothing else that we might call 'real'.

Because there is no fixed centre, there should no longer be any limits on what it is possible to think or believe. We should be allowed and able to think literally anything. Derrida maintains that when we realize that 'truth' and 'falsehood' are simply wrong distinctions to make, we can be more playful and flexible about the way we think. He suggests that ideas of truth and falsehood are just a destructive and harmful exercise of power and therefore we must stop considering everything in life, culture and thought in relation to absolute truth. To fail to do so is, for Derrida, oppressive and immoral.

A summary of Derrida's argument

We can summarize Derrida's argument like this:

1. Absolutes once provided foundations for everything. These absolutes come from God.
2. Derrida does not believe in God and therefore does not believe in absolutes either.
3. There is no possibility of certainty in life.
4. There are no intrinsic rights and wrongs in life.
5. To still think in terms of absolutes or rights and wrongs is oppressive and unjust.

New tools for new ways of thinking

From this argument Derrida concludes that we need new tools in order to think in new ways. He believes that traditional thought and language are oppressive, but that we are so wrapped up in them that we cannot see our way clear. Hence we need to develop tools that do away with such thought and language. He says that this is not just an academic exercise, but our *ethical* responsibility. Derrida claims that we must explode oppressive power regimes, among which he believes Christianity and Christian beliefs about God to be paramount.

In his search for new tools to explode traditional language and thought, Derrida says that any new tools *must* exclude absolutes from the start, because absolutes limit total freedom. For Derrida this is the most unethical act of all. He maintains that our most fundamental right is that of total freedom.

Derrida on history

Here are a few additional, less critical, points for those who want to think a bit further:

Derrida says that history is traditionally thought to be determined by Being (for which read 'God'). In other words, God guarantees history. There was a beginning that he created and there is an end to which he is working. Derrida sees this fact as responsible for most human optimism and ideas about progress. For example, science is based on the fact that there are true things to be discovered and goals towards which we can work.

Derrida, however, believes that this optimistic idea of history is precisely what stops people thinking radical new thoughts. The assumptions we pick up from history, he says, are inherently oppressive. For Derrida the fact that people *can and do* think radical new thoughts refutes this oppressive version of history and, of course, any absolute Being or God behind history. Derrida's idea of *play* or *flexibility* therefore completely denies the possibility of absolutes or of God.

This brief summary shows why Derrida believes we need new tools for thinking and writing. His big contribution is *deconstruction.* But what does the word mean and how is deconstruction supposed to work?

A bluffers' guide to deconstruction

Derrida starts, as we have seen, with the assumption that absolutes are a bad idea. They are really only the exercise of power. What then should we do with a text that claims to offer total solutions or overarching explanations of the world, such as the Bible?

Derrida goes on to suggest that if you look hard enough, sooner or later a text will contradict itself. This self-contradiction shows that the text is *constructed.* That is, a text is a work which is designed to have a particular manipulating effect on the reader but which cannot work its magic seamlessly without revealing its hand. Derrida says that *all* texts do this and all texts are written for the purpose of exercising power. By examining these supposedly self-contradicting parts of a text, deconstructionists claim to be able to spot the manipulation of the reader. This act of examination is what Derrida calls deconstruction. He claims that by deconstructing texts it is possible to expose harmful social conditioning.

By supposedly showing that a text cannot prevent itself from being self-contradictory and thus spotting the manipulation of the reader, the deconstructionist then claims to empower any social group who consider themselves to have been previously suppressed by a text or set of texts. Hence contemporary literary studies often focus on groups who have traditionally considered themselves disenfranchised – such as women, ethnic minorities, and homosexuals. The field is dominated by a host of so-called 'new readings' of texts – feminist deconstructions, subversive gay readings of Shakespeare, and the like.

If any text contradicts itself when you twist it hard enough, the deconstructionist maintains, any claim to truth will also contradict itself. This is why Derrida says that a text does not have a single or key meaning, indeed it cannot. Instead he says that all statements produce an explosion of varied and contradictory meanings, all of which are equally valid. Meanings do not have to agree. They can be mutually exclusive and still valuable because the value of the text lies not in determining the intention of the author but in allowing the text to express meaning of our own.

Deconstruction started to move out of the literary ghetto when people started defining things other than writing as 'texts'. Deconstructionists claim that our only access to the world is through language and therefore *everything in the world* is a construction with the potential for an explosion of meanings. A piece of music may be a text, a technical drawing or a work of art may be a text, a city may be a text. The world is a text. All these texts, it is claimed, contain multiple meanings and stories, just like the literary text. And these stories do not have to agree with each other.

At the most radical edge of the Postmodern debate people are treated as texts. It is claimed that we are mere vessels full of stories and meanings. Like the literary text, these meanings do not have to agree with each other. Early deconstruction challenged communication of meaning. More recent deconstruction challenges the ability to live as a coherent person. Granted, the existence and prevalence of sin means that we will not be perfect until we reach heaven, but the lie of deconstruction is that we may *never* aspire to coherent meaning, value or communication. The ultimate end of relativism is not only that the objective world collapses, leaving individuals as the only arbiter of value, but that finally the individual collapses as well, leaving a fractured ego. Deconstructionists say that it is impossible to decide what it means to be human.

A concise summary of deconstruction

1. There are no such things as absolutes or total solutions.
2. Any text (especially ones that claim to have total solutions) must contain contradictions.
3. Spotting contradictions shows the text to be fallible, and hence stops it having oppressive power.
4. Deconstruction is the name given to the act of spotting such alleged contradictions.
5. The closer you examine a text, the more contradictions and potential meanings you find – there is an explosion of meanings, all of which are valid.
6. Everything can be treated as a text – including the whole world and people.

Some questions

1. Is any of this relevant to the student Diane?
2. Is Derrida right or wrong? Why?
3. What are the flaws in the argument? Is there anything you can affirm in the argument?
4. How might deconstruction affect people's understanding of God, Scripture and ourselves?

A Christian response to deconstruction

Deconstruction is corrosive. It sees attacking truth claims as an ethical duty. It is anti-truth, in theory and in practice. In fairness we should note that if you don't believe in God then there is no reason not to be a deconstructionist, but the end result of deconstruction even makes some card-carrying Postmodernists uneasy. Here are some pointers to responding to deconstruction.

Spot the underlying assumptions

As with much Postmodern theory, deconstruction depends on certain premises which are assumed but not explored. We can immediately spot several. The first is that God does not exist. The second premise is that absolute truth is the same thing as repressive Western thought. Thirdly, communication isn't really possible. A fourth assumption is that no genuine authority exists, or could communicate itself if it did.

The key point is the first one. The deconstructionist position cannot accept the presence of God. In fact it dismisses God as a prior assumption before starting the task of deconstruction. Deconstruction denies the possibility of revelation or of God creating and safeguarding human communication. Postmodernists see 'oppressive' Western thought and Judeo-Christian values as the same thing. The result is that they can blame all of society's ills on a Judeo-Christian commitment to absolute truth. For the deconstructionist the idea of God *revealing* truth is the ultimate evil to be fought because revelation limits creative thinking. It is seen as the greatest tool of oppression. We should note, however, that the denial of revelation must itself be an absolute in order for deconstruction to work. As we shall see, deconstruction's own internal presuppositions are contradictory.

Deconstruction itself can be a power game

While some groups may indeed have been disenfranchised in the past, deconstruction finds in minority groups a useful starting point. It works best when it is championing a cause. It often presupposes that such a cause *must* exist – there must be groups who will benefit from its services. It is virtually guaranteed to find them. Deconstruction sees itself, then, as a tool for liberation. This liberation comes from rebelling against existing power structures, especially Christianity. Where such structures are hard to find, they are frequently imagined. For example, it is almost impossible to argue sensibly about liberation from a loving Creator God, but if you dress him in the garb of oppressive Western colonialism, then he becomes an easy target.

Deconstruction depends on taking things out of context

Deconstruction depends on finding minute points in a text that seem to say the opposite to the main message. This almost invariably means taking small portions, even individual words or syllables, out of context. But this is simply not the way we read texts. Deconstruction has a warped way of reading. To say that real meaning *must* flow from a divorce between a text and its context, or that real meaning is apparent only at a minute deconstructive level, or that real meaning must be the opposite to what a text ostensibly says, is not only anti-knowledge, but arrogant in the extreme. Deconstruction effectively claims that its followers are the only ones with the new tools who can creatively approach a text to discover its real value.

Moreover, deconstructionists are not necessarily coherent in their application of the principle. It is quite possible to produce 'Christian readings' of texts in conflict with anti-Christian ones. Anyone can take something out of context and make it say what we want. There is nothing to say that we shouldn't. Most deconstructionists, however, would roundly disclaim such 'absolutist readings' but, by their own admission, have no grounds for doing so.

Deconstruction denies humanity

Pushed to its logical extreme, deconstruction breaks down

ideas of what it means to be human. Many people are now freely saying that there is no such thing as humanity, no one idea of what it means to be human. When we cease to understand that we are made in God's image for a relationship with him, then we cease to have any right foundations for understanding ourselves. Some go so far as to say that we are simply in an indeterminate state in our evolution, not human but *mutants*. Others, however, are questioning where this leaves human dignity, identity, morality or society.

Clearly, the vital challenge for Christians is to recover our doctrine of humanity. We *are* created in God's image. We possess inherent dignity as his creation. We *can* communicate accurately because he created speech and meaning. We *do* have a moral sense because he defines right and wrong according to his own character and he makes them known to us.

Deconstruction misunderstands liberty

Deconstruction also has a wrong definition of freedom or liberty. We might feel liberated by standing on a cliff thinking that we can fly, but when we flap our arms and leap, we discover that this isn't real freedom at all. There are limits built into our humanity. They are clear for all to see, regardless of how much we would like to deny that they are there. To proclaim that the highest expression of human rights is total freedom, freedom from any restrictions, freedom from God, not only flies in the face of the truth, but is the ultimate philosophical example of the emperor having no clothes on. We can proclaim our ultimate liberty to our hearts' content, but that doesn't make it possible, let alone good.

In the whole-hearted pursuit of liberty we have become blinded to the issues of truth and freedom. If we are liberated from the truth, the last thing we are is free. Jesus claimed time and again to tell the truth because he *is* the Truth. Which is why in John 8 Jesus claims that freedom comes from knowing him and obeying his teaching. The ascended Jesus sent the Holy Spirit to indwell Christians, and the Holy Spirit is the Spirit of Truth. In other words, believing in absolute truth and living in freedom are not mutually exclusive, as Derrida would claim. The exact opposite is the case – believing truth is the *only* thing that sets us free. Those who deny not only God's revealed truth but any concept of truth at all refuse to accept the world as it really is. This is not freedom, it is blindness.

We need to encourage people to ask what they think they are being liberated *from*, and liberated *for*. Deconstruction wants freedom from all limits, but do we really want to be free from being human? We might add that while deconstruction does a very good job at destroying any sense of value, it puts nothing in its place except a void.

Deconstruction misunderstands thinking itself

Deconstruction values radical new thought for its own sake. This, too, is flawed, in three ways. In the first place, it has no reason to do so, as it denies the validity of communication, or indeed of coherent thinking. Secondly, it is of little use in making decisions, as *any* radical thought is proclaimed to be equally valid – even conflicting ones. There are no criteria for deciding which is of greater political or ethical value. Derrida himself says this must infinitely delay decision. Even some of his fans find this difficult to accept, and some writers are currently exploring the idea of a theory of deconstruction that still allows ethical decisions to be made. A third flaw is that there is frequently little idea of what constitutes radical thought, except that it is what breaks up the *status quo*.

People behave as though they believe in absolutes.

Plenty of people believe in God. Many people believe in absolute standards of morality and behaviour. The deconstructionist says this demonstrates social conditioning, but there is no good reason to suppose that it does. It is just as valid to say that we are just made that way. It is difficult to apply the social conditioning argument across cultures where similar taboos or ideas of conscience have developed independently. In addition, we should maintain that this deconstructionist reading is one that its adherents cannot possibly verify or hold in higher regard than any other opinion, if they are to be consistent. To deny the right to believe in absolutes is, itself, imperialist and oppressive.

How does this affect Diane?

Diane raises many of the issues we saw with Mike in Chapter 1. The Classics department may be academically impressive but Diane faces people who proclaim that the individual is the only arbiter of value, that we can behave as we like because there is no one to say otherwise and that there are no external criteria for meaning or moral behaviour. There is no God either to guarantee communication or to offend.

There are two ways in which this affects Diane. The first and most important is in the moral arena. She is surrounded by teaching that believes there are no moral absolutes. She is having to deal with behaviour that lives this out in flagrant and disgusting ways. This is far from uncommon both at university and beyond. Diane needs help to stand against those who believe there is no foundation to life. She needs encouragement to be a strong disciple and a good witness. In this sort of environment there are many discouragements to stand for Christ, and it would be easy for her to live a closet Christian existence, even if she didn't get tempted into immoral behaviour herself.

Diane might also need help to realize that there are more important things in life than prospects. If the most exciting things are happening in classes from which her faith excludes her, she may have to face the hard fact that it is better to be faithful to God than to get the highest degree. She may well face moral pressure to limit any criticism of Derrida or not to state any values that go against the prevailing culture.

The gay and gender issues in the department bear all the hallmarks of the spirit of the age. Promiscuity usually means a low view of human dignity and reduces relationships to sex. Diane needs to see that this is not 'being radical' or experiencing genuine freedom. Indeed, this behaviour denies the value of people. Helping Diane to maintain her Christian lifestyle and values in this department is crucial to helping her grow as a Christian. Clearly, she needs a lot of care and attention, as much of what the department is teaching is corrosive to godliness.

Secondly, it would help Diane academically just to gain a handle on what the theory is all about and how it affects our thoughts about God, the Bible and ourselves. If it is possible to help her grasp what the Bible says about our humanity, this would give her a yardstick with which to evaluate her university teaching. It would also help if Diane were encouraged to understand the assumptions behind deconstruction. She would benefit from realizing that it is often a power game and from seeing that deconstruction depends on taking things out of context. This would help her to understand the implications of deconstruction for humanity, liberty and thinking.

Chapter 3

How Do We Know What Is Important?

The question of value

The aspects of contemporary culture discussed in the previous two chapters are hard to get to grips with. But they are important. I have heard these ideas described by influential thinkers and academics as 'the most important thought in the world today'. These thinkers are self-consciously trying to design the future after their own image, promoting the things they think are important, attacking almost all traditional Christian values. It is with the question of *value* that these ideas about authority finally come down to earth.

So many ideas around in the culture today suggest that there is no such thing as value. That it is impossible for us to say that anything has lasting importance. Yet we yearn for meaning and significance. No matter what the apostles of Darwin teach about us being nothing more than a delivery package for DNA, there is a deep desire to know that we *mean* something and that the world and what goes on in it is more than a cosmic accident.

The question of what we hold to be valuable and why we do so therefore cuts to the heart of our identity. Consistent relativists cannot say that anything has lasting value at all. For them nothing lasts and everything is only valuable in its own culture, if at all. It is to the question of how we know what is important or valuable that we turn in this chapter. I believe the question of value to be one of the most important ways to helping people see the bankruptcy of a lot of contemporary theory and popular culture. If people think there is a reason for placing value on something, reason that is more than just personal preference, then they cannot be relativists.

Some questions

Pause for a moment and ask yourself the following questions:

1. What do we mean when we say we 'value' something or someone?
2. What events, experiences, beliefs and objects do we place most value on?
3. Why and how do we value some things above others?
4. When faced with a choice between two options, what criteria help us to decide between them?
5. Is 'value' purely a question of taste or personal preference, or is it more than these?

People have stopped asking this kind of question. But when they *are* asked, most people see that the answers are important. Indeed, the answers are key to our identity, our behaviour and all our decision-making. We are all products of the decisions we make. Some decisions are comparatively insignificant (What shall I wear today? What shall I eat?) but many are huge in their scope and consequences (What dreams shall I pursue? Whom shall I marry? What will have priority in my life's ambitions?). The decisions we take radically affect the people we become. All our decisions depend on us believing and acting as though some things are more valuable and more worth pursuing than others. But few of us consciously think about why we decide the way we do about valuable things. When we do think about it, it is not always easy to discern why we act as we do or where answers to these questions may be found.

Case study

Frank is an artist and sculptor. One day you meet briefly at church and ask how his work is going. He tells you that he is being challenged by the question of whether there is such a thing as high art and low art, in painting, sculpture or film.

'You see, so many of the values by which people seem to have tried to distinguish between high and low art seem to be purely subjective when you look at them closely. Matthew Arnold said something was high art if it aimed at representing the best that a culture had to offer, if it was almost spiritual in scope. But his definitions of "spiritual" and "cultural excellence" seem to be pretty limited and self-serving when you actually look at them. He seems to define "the best" as "the best as Matthew Arnold would like it to be".'

You ask Frank why this particular question is engaging him.

He replies: 'It seems such a small step for many artists today to go from saying that there is no such thing as high art and low art, to saying that there are no criteria of value for us to decide between them, to saying that there are no criteria of value in life as a whole. They say we have to dismiss claims that something is high art or valuable art because the claim simply reveals prejudice on behalf of the artist or the critic. Nothing to do with value, only with the power to impose their personal preferences on us.'

'What does that mean about truth?'

'Well, of course it means that it is impossible to determine what sort of music is better or worse, what films are better or worse, what TV is good or bad on any basis of truth. But, even more than that, at the end of the day it means that no discussion of value is really valid because it all comes back to truth claims in the end. I feel the argument must be wrong. I mean, how do we decide how to act or what to like and dislike? But I can't quite see how it is wrong. I know quite a lot of artists whose whole work is starting to revolve around death or nihilism. It seems like they have junked the idea of anything being valuable and are left with a big vacuum inside them.'

Some more questions

Before we go deeper into the question of value, it is worth pondering your answers to the following questions:

1. How would you describe the issues that Frank is wrestling with?
2. What underlying assumptions from relativism and pluralism do they contain?
3. Why might these sorts of ideas affect people enough to change the artwork they produce?
4. What do these ideas say about their identity and personal values?
5. How might you help Frank think through the issues?

The theory bit: *Walter Benjamin*

One crucial essay that seeks to explore the way we value things, and how our ability to make value judgments is changing, is Walter Benjamin's (pronounced Varl-ter Ben-ya-meen) superb and provocative 'The Work Of Art In The Age Of Its Mechanical Reproduction'. Unlike some of the other essays explored in this book, this one is comparatively easy reading and well worth getting hold of.

Our consumer-centred shopping culture is closely connected to a lot of trendy theories and ideas which deify the individual. We define ourselves not so much by who we are as by what we buy. '*Tescos ergo sum*', as one wit put it – I shop therefore I am. Benjamin sets out to show that the demands of a mass consumerist culture cause us to lose our ability to make good critical judgments on questions of value. His argument is as follows.

Technology, Benjamin begins, has reached the stage where a work of art is perfectly mechanically reproducible. The mass market is less concerned with the perfection of a work of art than with its accessibility. However, even the most perfect reproduction loses the setting, purpose and history of the original as soon as the reproduction is made. The reproduction may be a perfect one, but it cannot have the original's aura of authenticity because it does not serve the function of the original. Its value is thus depreciated, according to Benjamin. He uses the example of an artwork that was originally designed for some kind of worship. As soon as it is removed from its place in temple or church, then it sacrifices its authenticity.

Secondly, he argues, mechanical reproduction therefore exchanges unique existence for plural copies. When we satisfy the mass demand to make art widely available, we sacrifice uniqueness and permanence. For Benjamin the most important example of this is film, which he believes is extremely transitory in its value.

Thirdly, film and TV are so popular that we adjust our tastes accordingly. Hence Benjamin thinks that we have started to believe that reality itself is, or should be, transitory. We care little for the tradition that makes a work of art unique. We want it all now, regardless of the value of what we get. Hence we have actually given the work of art an entirely new function – to be exhibited purely for instant gratification. This, says Benjamin, is illustrated by the fact that captions have become obligatory. It is necessary to have an explanation to bridge the gap between the purpose of the unique original and the purpose of the reproduction.

Benjamin's fourth point is that film and TV have the appearance of giving us raw experience of life straight in the face. They seem to be unmediated, but this isn't the case. We see what the director wants us to see. Film pretends to have the authenticity of unique experience, but is in fact just a lifelike reproduction of reality. Hence, when we make value judgments about a film or TV – was it good or bad and why? – we do so without any real ability to distinguish value judgments about things that matter from ones about things that don't. We shouldn't be surprised at someone telling us that TV rots the brain. Benjamin's contribution is to do so in a highly thoughtful, clever way. He shows that TV and film effectively prevent us from having any verifiable criteria on which to form value judgments. As an aside he comments that film is fragmented in the way it is put together and the way it is presented. As a result we become used to the idea that the way we receive experience and make judgments should also be fragmented.

As his next point Benjamin says that because we have lost our critical faculties, we have replaced art with a commodity for consumption, and we have replaced critical value judgments with the cult of the movie star. Benjamin's key conclusion is that when we lose our critical faculties, we then start to value everything uncritically. A vicious circle ensues. Film and TV makers produce material to appeal to this uncritical market. The consumer society creates the demand that it then satisfies. In the process it removes or fudges questions of value.

Benjamin adds that the fragmentary nature of film and TV ensures that we consume powerful representations of the world in sound-bites and rapid images, rather than with thoughtful purpose. The more the social significance of the work of art decreases, the more we tend to enjoy it uncritically, because we become more and more used to the conventions of TV and film. As the fish is uncritical of the water in which it swims, so we have become uncritical of our TV environment. The way we now participate in mass culture is overwhelmingly superficial, because mass demand settles for low common denominators, instant gratification and short concentration spans.

A summary of Benjamin's argument

1. Everything is perfectly reproducible but the act of reproduction devalues things.
2. Reproduction exchanges uniqueness and permanence for plurality and transience.
3. We change our tastes accordingly to enjoy transient things uncritically.
4. As a result we rapidly lose our ability to exercise value judgments – particularly when watching TV or films.
5. The end result is that we lose our critical faculties altogether. We begin to value everything uncritically.
6. Consumer society then satisfies the demand for worthless commodities.
7. As we consume these commodities, life becomes overwhelmingly superficial.

A Christian response to Benjamin

Benjamin's argument clearly contains a great deal of truth and sound observation. The development of mass culture does indeed alienate us from ourselves. True reality and representations of reality on TV often differ hugely from each other, though we may well be unable to distinguish between them. Benjamin says that when we are unable to make judgments about the world, we destroy our identities. And through the power of Hollywood we experience this self-destruction as aesthetic pleasure and banal escapism.

If Benjamin is right (and mostly I think he is), then we live in a society that has downgraded any sense of value. The leisure industry makes us settle for the lowest common denominator, causing us to drink it all in uncritically. The end product is yet greater consumption and the market for yet more products.

How should we respond when we meet issues like these? We may meet them in discussions of contemporary issues, as in the case study. We may do so in university courses if we are students. But we all do so every time we switch on our television and try to make sense of what it tells us about the world.

Understanding why questions of value are important

In much discussion today the question of high and low art is crucial. You may have met it when your children's English teachers have opted for populist modern texts instead of classics. You might have found the issue powerfully presented to you when you visited a modern art gallery. The key thing to understand is that many believe that there is no distinction between high art and low art, because they believe there are no criteria of value to decide what should go under each category – indeed, that there is no agreed ground for deciding what is valuable and what is not in any circumstance.

The question of values is vital because it is not finally about personal preferences but about morals. Some things are overwhelmingly important. Some things are true. The judgments we make about these things matter to all. We must be able to decide in which areas of life we *must* make value judgments, and which can be treated purely as a matter of preference.

The current debate over values often makes three false assumptions, all of which flow from the uncritical acceptance of relativism.

The first faulty assumption is that either there are valid ways to decide the case between high art and low art, or there can be no valid criteria for making any value judgments about anything at all, ever. Notice how the question is unfairly polarized, revealing a second assumption. We are forced to say either that we believe in totally enforced absolutes in all areas of life, belief and behaviour (i.e. fascism), or that we believe that all matters of value can only ever be relative.

A third and very common assumption is that discussion of high and low art should be concerned more with technical merit than with moral value – that is, we should make value judgments according to how well a work is presented rather than according to the value of its content.

How should we approach questions of value?

How then should we approach questions of value as Christians? Our starting point is, of course, our understanding of God. We believe that God is a moral being who makes moral choices according to his character. He embodies truth and righteousness. Therefore it is possible for us to make moral decisions on the basis of truth, knowing right from wrong, because God has revealed himself and his purposes. But God also has aesthetic sensibilities. He enjoys creating and delights in beauty. He not only distinguishes purity from sin in the moral realm, he also distinguishes attractiveness from ugliness in the aesthetic realm. In giving us real power to create things, a power modelled after his own creative nature, God gives us the option to exercise our creativity in ways that delight or disgust him. In both the moral and the aesthetic arenas it is both possible and vital to make value judgments. It is possible because God himself does and it is vital because this is his creation and not ours. Being made and owned by God places on us the responsibility to value the things that God values and to hate the things that he hates.

Many falsely caricature Christians, saying that if we believe in God, and God's values and revelation of truth, we must therefore believe that there are absolute standards on all matters at all times. This is unbiblical. We do not have to locate a biblical standpoint on every minute detail in order to make right choices. Please don't mishear me. The Bible is vital for our daily lives and decision-making. But the caricature suggests that anyone who believes the Bible must have an absolute opinion on everything, down to the level of what colour socks to wear. We fall into the trap of the second point above – either we must believe that all matters, however minute, are absolutely dictated to us, or we should enjoy a total free-for-all.

Christians *do* believe in absolutes in many areas of life and belief. God has revealed much that is true that we are to obey for his glory and our good. However, Christians are *also* relativists in many areas, either because God has not specifically spoken about them or because he allows us to make wisdom decisions about them based on our knowledge of him. Some matters *are* in the area of personal preference, but not everything, as the relativists maintain.

It is because Christians have an absolute standard in the character of God and a reliable guide in the Bible that we are the *only* ones with a dependable yardstick about what we must hold absolutely and what we may take to be relative. Nobody else has such a guide. With the question of high art and low art we should accept, provided the work is not morally shameful, that this is an area in which we may exercise preference. To take the next step of saying there are therefore no criteria of value is to confuse value and preference.

The discussion often reaches conclusions that are a vague smokescreen rather than specific. I recall a class in which the theoretical conclusion was that any possible expression of sexuality is valuable. All sexuality should be a matter of personal preference, and personal preference is worthwhile in and of itself. To earth the discussion in a specific example, I asked about paedophilia. Everyone agreed that paedophilia is wrong – including the relativists! Asking a specific question often helps people see the difficulties with underlying ideas. Using extreme examples like this is not always helpful, but it does show that there are some areas of life in which even the most committed Postmodernist feels the need to make value judgments.

The issue of authenticity

One of the heart-cries of our society is for authenticity. We don't want to discover that we are merely an empty shell into which the aspirations of the media industry have been poured. Authenticity depends on how we decide what to value, and on there being at least some absolutes in life. Without absolutes there are no grounds for giving any meaning or significance to any of our actions, or our lives. The quest for authenticity demonstrates a desire to invest in things that are true and worthwhile. In a world searching for significance, the question of authenticity is a good one for Christians to use to point to The Truth. We can show that real authenticity is only possible when we have the relationship with God for which we were created. Our generation is forgetting what it means to be authentically human. The theorists are saying that there is *nothing* authentic about being human. They could not be more wrong.

The ways we think

Perhaps Benjamin's biggest challenge is to show how easily we accept the world uncritically. We do so because we have divorced our critical faculties from our moral ones. It is much easier to emphasize personal preference if we ignore any overarching moral standards. In my work with Christian students I have discovered that even Christians can think this way. We may know that Christ has saved us and that God has revealed himself, and yet somehow fail to see the moral obligation this puts on our lives and behaviour. Often this means we have been taught about God's love but not that we should obey God and fear him.

What is the link between our critical and moral faculties? It is closely related to being concerned to obey God's commands. We desire to discern right from wrong in order to please him. This is hard to encourage people to do in a me-centred age. But it is also hard to do because we are not used to thinking Christianly about the world and the way it is mediated to us. We need to have our minds transformed by God's Spirit through his Word and to sharpen up our transformed minds by using them. The areas in which we are to use our Christian minds are obvious – academic study, film and TV, peer relationships, to name just a few. Benjamin argues that society has forced us to turn off our critical faculties. When we understand that these faculties are linked to our moral obedience of God, we see that not only must we turn them back on, but we need to use them to evaluate and change our lives in line with God's revealed truth. This is particularly vital for young people and students, the programme-makers and opinion-formers of tomorrow.

How does this relate to Frank?

Finally, what about Frank? First he needs to spot that there is a difference between preference and value. His contemporaries may (vigorously) contend that there are no grounds for making value judgments, but they have no case to say that their non-values are any more plausible than his commitment to truth.

When he has grasped this distinction, it is also important for him to recognize that some areas of life are subjective, but not all by any means. Frank must not let others polarize him out of the discussion simply by labelling him as a fascist.

Frank knows fellow artists who are sinking in a mire of nihilism. These are obvious examples of the personal consequences of lack of value – potent emptiness and apathy. The pragmatic effects in real lives might open up the chance to discuss whether there is something wrong with the art course's basic assumptions. Once again it is the often unspoken assumptions of relativism that inform this debate, and they need to be exposed. It is important to realize that this nihilism is not just a result of some bad philosophy, it is the result of an immoral understanding about the world and ourselves. If we fail to see that relativism is immoral in its anti-God suppositions, then we will have no answer to its dreadful consequences.

It might help Frank to understand why questions of value are important. This will involve spotting false assumptions through asking specific questions about relativistic art theory and checking the answers against what God has revealed as being valuable. It would be a further benefit to Frank to understand what God has said about authentic humanity. This would include understanding that God is concerned about the way that we think – and that Postmodern assumptions about our minds are deliberately anti-Christ.

Chapter 4

What Does It Mean to Be a Person?

The fourth aspect of contemporary theory we will consider is that of gender. Much of this aspect of Postmodernism comes from feminism, and is quite complicated. The essay we will discuss is the hardest of the five and I don't recommend that you try to read it unless you have a specific interest in this area.

Some of the most potent and anti-Christian scholarship is coming from the area of gender studies. In particular, the quest for female equality has been transformed into a quest to deconstruct gender and promote homosexuality. What does this mean in practice? Consider the following case study.

Case study

Imagine you lead a church home group.

One home-group night the members arrive as usual. Then the doorbell rings and Sophie is there. Having enjoyed one career, Sophie is now retraining in nursing. She loves helping others and finds nursing a great way to exercise the gifts God has given her for caring for those in need. On this particular night, however, Sophie's eyes are tear-stained. It is not hard to tell that something is wrong. Gently steering her away from the rest of the group, you ask if she is all right.

'We had a terrible nursing class today,' she says. 'I felt so demeaned and dirty but I just didn't know what to do.'

'What happened?' you ask.

'It was a class designed to help us cope with any situation. I thought it would be helpful, but it wasn't. The class leader told us that nurses have to lose all their inhibitions in order to avoid being sickened or offended by some of the things we might meet on the wards.'

You wonder what could be so unhelpful about that sort of class.

'The way they went about it,' Sophie continues, 'was to make us all ...' she flushes bright red, 'well ... touch each other inappropriately.' She hangs her head. 'I just didn't know what to do. Then we were all told to lick each other.'

'Did you take part?' you ask.

She nods. 'I didn't know what else to do. But now I feel horrible. I did object at first.'

'And what happened?'

'I was shouted at by practically the whole group. There was one much younger woman in particular who told me that I was insulting her. I wasn't trying to insult her, but she said that if I didn't approve of the class then I was demeaning her personal sexual choices and scorning a vital human right of choice. I couldn't believe how quickly it changed from a nursing lesson to an attack on me. I guess that's why I joined in. Some of the literature we were considering said that there is no such thing as gay or straight anyway. That there is only personal preference.'

Over the next few weeks you and the church pastor counsel Sophie to put in a formal complaint with the nursing college.

She is forcefully rebuffed. One senior member of staff comments that this is a new century and that nursing has no place for antiquated attitudes or people who won't show a bit of team spirit. He wonders aloud if Sophie is simply too old to retrain and whether she should try another 'less demanding' line of work.

Sophie is worried that, by raising the issue with the college, she will be unfairly marked down. Since the class she has also found herself socially rejected.

'I never knew it was a crime to raise questions about gender or gay issues,' she says. 'But that is how I feel now. And next term there will be some teaching about sexuality on our course. I am really worried that I have already seen what that is going to be like. I want to behave as a Christian, but I don't quite know how I will survive.'

Some questions

It is helpful to pause and reflect on Sophie's situation. Try listing the issues that she is struggling with.

1. What underlying assumptions from relativism and pluralism do they contain?
2. How would you help her to think them through?
3. What sort of effect might each have on her life and witness?
4. Is it possible to challenge an environment like this or should she give up her ambitions to be a nurse?

The theory bit: *Judith Butler*

You may think this case study is so extreme that it couldn't possibly be based on reality. Tragically, you would be wrong. The incident powerfully demonstrates that what may start off in the realm of theory very quickly has implications for morality and behaviour. Sophie was rapidly drawn into something that she knew was wrong because everyone else blurred the lines about good and evil and submitted her to intense peer pressure.

I find it particularly interesting to hear of examples of this sort of thing in areas such as nursing. We might think that nursing would be pragmatic, dealing in facts and procedures. Perhaps it often is. But nursing and other medical and scientific professions are now as deeply in the grip of Postmodernism as the most radical literary theory. This is because, while the claims of contemporary culture might not alter a medical diagnosis or cure, they certainly affect the attitudes, values and morals of the practitioners.

In the case study it also seems that there may be some specific teaching going on that challenges our ideas about gender and sexuality. This sort of writing and thinking is known as 'gender theory'. In some spheres it is huge currency. You will meet it if you are a student in most arts subjects. You will be confronted by it in some form if you are in medicine or an allied profession. You cannot avoid it if you turn on the TV, let alone if you are a media professional. We only have to reflect on the amount of sexuality in the media to see this is true.

Much of the theory is complicated, including the essay I have chosen to discuss: 'Subjects of Sex/Gender/Desire' by Judith Butler. It would take a book in itself to deal in any depth with Butler, and even then she would probably maintain that a man couldn't explain or critique her work adequately. I shall, nevertheless, try to summarize her key points that bear on our subject.

1. Male society represses women

Butler's essay starts off with five quotes. Each one makes the point that gender is not inherent to us as people but is constructed by our environment. For example: 'The category of sex is the political category that founds society as heterosexual' (Monique Wittig). Her point is that society defines gender – masculinity or femininity – in order to keep women oppressed. Sex, for Butler, is a political act of domination of women by men. She believes that men have created the whole system to keep things this way. She says that this act of tyranny includes law which is designed to keep men on top, social taboos that make women believe that they have a lower status than men, and even language itself which she says is male-dominated in the very way it is made up.

2. Traditional Feminism does not free women

Butler is not convinced by traditional Feminism. She defines traditional Feminism as the attempt to find a means, within law, language and society, of freeing women from male bonds. The Feminists tried to find words which could be used for women and by women that weren't already dominated by men.

But, predictably, Butler thinks that the whole of society is so male-dominated that there are simply no words or laws that do not control women. She says that the judicial system has made it legal to think in certain ways, and has suppressed other ways of thinking. And all the legal ways are male. This has left women without a language of their own. Femininity can then only be defined as what is non-male.

3. Ideas about gender oppress women

Butler says that the notion of gender is one of the ways in which society oppresses women. Traditional Feminism sought to recover femininity as a gender. According to Butler this is impossible because the whole concept of feminine gender is a male one anyway. In other words, while sex is biological – we are male and female – gender is constructed and imposed upon women by men. We grow up thinking that we are masculine or feminine because male society has told us to.

4. Butler's answer is to deny gender

Butler believes that the only way to reverse this situation is not to try to reclaim femininity but rather to deny the whole concept of gender. For her 'man' and 'woman' are irrelevant labels that only describe the oppression of women. She suggests that the labels can be deconstructed to show that there is no concept of masculine or feminine or of moral right and wrong in sexuality. Instead she teaches that there are as many different genders as there are people. We should therefore all be free to try whatever expression of our identity and our sexuality that we feel drawn to. As in our case study, if anyone denies us this right, then Butler maintains that they are oppressing us and denying us our ultimate freedom as people.

5. This leads to a crisis of identity

Butler then questions the whole idea of identity. She suggests that our identity is not a stable thing. Stability was found only under the old system, which Butler links closely to heterosexuality and male oppression. She wishes to find a new identity that she claims cannot be found under an oppressive heterosexual understanding of who we are. In a comment on Wittig she says: 'the binary [i.e. heterosexual] restriction on sex serves the reproductive aims of a system of compulsory heterosexuality … occasionally [Wittig] claims that the overthrow of compulsory heterosexuality will inaugurate a true humanism of "the person" freed from the shackles of sex.' Or in other words, heterosexuality is repressive, and we can only be free if we are free from traditional ideas about sex and gender, of which heterosexuality is the worst. Masculine culture is seen as oppressive tyranny or sexual metanarrative that can only be overthrown by overthrowing identity with it. She strikes at the heart of what it means to be a person, effectively suggesting that the only possible moral position is to be homosexual. She believes that homosexuality allows people to deliberately live outside the norms and thus escape domination.

6. Butler does not think her position is open to question

Butler attacks many important things and tries to make immorality normative. She also powerfully states that it is impossible to debate with anyone else on the nature of personhood. She believes there is simply no common ground on which to debate. With this slick move she says that it is not possible to challenge what she says because she is the champion of freedom. She dismisses any attempt to gainsay her on the grounds that there is no common humanity from which we can debate. She comments: 'In other words, "the coherence" and "continuity" of "the person" are not logical or analytical features of personhood, but, rather, socially instituted and maintained norms of intelligibility.'

All of which is a convoluted way of saying that there is no one, true right understanding of what it means to be human. Being human can mean whatever each individual would like.

A summary of Butler's argument

1. Male society represses women.
2. Traditional Feminism does not free women.
3. Ideas about gender oppress women.
4. The answer is to deny gender.
5. This leads to a crisis of identity.
6. Butler does not think her position is open to question.

More questions

Let us pause again and consider some pertinent questions:

1. Is any of this discussion of Butler's theory relevant to Sophie's situation?
2. Is Butler right or wrong? Why?
3. What are the flaws in the argument?
4. Is there anything you can affirm in the argument?
5. How does Butler's argument challenge the way the Bible describes us?

A Christian response to Butler

Some Postmodernists suggest that there is no right idea of what it means to be human. This sections shows why. It is an attempt to affirm any identity we wish for ourselves – in fact, a new form of Babel. You can read the account of the tower of Babel in Genesis 11. What happened at that time was that the sin that entered the world with Adam and Eve had spread to the whole of mankind. Our whole race stood up in rebellion against God, deciding that we would make ourselves great, that we would define our own identity and that we would dethrone him as our King. It was the ultimate quest for autonomy from God. Contemporary gender theory also attempts to produce the ultimate in human autonomy – total freedom to express whatever sort of gender we wish. And total freedom to believe that we are right and moral to do so.

I once attended a lecture in which it was taught that when gender is deconstructed we are free to construct for ourselves any form of sexuality that we find fulfilling. This is not only right, we were told, it is our moral duty, because by doing so we challenge the oppressive male regime under which we have been brought up. Once again I asked whether paedophilia is acceptable. There was an awkward pause before I was told that paedophilia is a provocative term that would hinder rather than aid discussion. The discussion moved swiftly on but the underlying assumption in this lecture was that even paedophilia was probably within the boundaries of acceptability. Indeed, some Postmodern writers are overtly saying just that, justifying it by claiming that paedophilia empowers children, giving them the right to refuse sexual favours to adults. This is chilling stuff. Butler's ideas are extremely dangerous.

Butler's argument is hard to get to grips with and is expressed in complicated language, but when we have done so it is not hard to counter. Let's consider a few points about the argument itself.

Butler presupposes her own conclusions

Butler begins by holding the position she sets out to prove. She tries to convince the reader along the way that she is arguing from universal principles that all accept, but she is not. It is worth pushing this sort of argument to see what it assumes before it starts. We should always ask what ideas lie behind something that seems to be unbiblical. In Butler's case her essay assumes at least the following four things: (1) that sex is political; (2) that the juridical system can only ever be male; (3) that language can only ever be male; and (4) that gender identity is culturally imposed. She assumes in addition that she is not open to contradiction. This is not acceptable either academically or morally, and yet the reader is expected to accept all of these assumptions before even beginning. On biblical grounds we must say that all are highly questionable.

Another question

Pause briefly and think how you would respond from the Bible to each of the above assumptions.

Butler holds an extreme relativist position

Butler at least has the courage to pursue relativism to its ultimate conclusion. She is right to say that relativism leads us to the view that there is no such thing as humanity. In the process she suggests that there is a complete breakdown of the terms 'male' and 'masculine' and 'female' and 'feminine'. According to her argument, we cannot really know who we are. We are all merely involved in a fruitless life-long experiment to discover our identity, even though we know that there are no meaningful answers to find. Or rather, the only meaningful answer is exactly what I want it to be.

Butler does a 180-degree U-turn on traditional morality

For Butler it is the homosexual position that has the moral high ground. While she maintains that it is impossible to say one gender is preferable to another, she also holds heterosexuality to be deeply suspect and repressive. Logically we ought to say that she cannot have it both ways.

Some implications of Butler's position

Butler assumes that it is no longer possible to hold common belief that is true for everyone. She applies pluralism and relativism to sexuality and identity. In the absence of any goal-posts that say what is right and wrong, the only things to go on are personal preference and feelings.

Moral criteria, in her argument, have been replaced by the idea of 'rights'. The campaign to have a variety of 'rights' officially recognized is one of the defining marks of our culture. Recognizing rights to freedom of belief or of speech is one thing, but the current concern about rights is a deeper matter. To have your concerns recognized by society as a right means being able to use the machinery of that society to wage war on those who disagree. If we have rights in this culture, then somebody else is wrong.

Butler writes for the right for women to be whatever they desire to be. I do not want to be heard to challenge the equality of the sexes, but Butler says that the only way to uphold women's rights is to knock down the whole notion of identity. Is this not a case of championing a right simply out of personal desire? I recently read a newspaper article on sexuality and gender. The article was cautiously positive about heterosexuality. I say 'cautiously' because it clearly felt that the overriding public perception is that any sexuality is now okay and it didn't wish to inflame the homosexual lobby. We have arrived, through the work of people like Butler, at a point in time and culture when we call right wrong and wrong right. All this flows from using relativism to pursue personal desire. Our personal wants and desires are frequently unholy.

Butler clearly thinks that it is impossible for people to be consistent. It is more important to go with our feelings of the moment. For her, the highest good is that I should express myself however I please. But consistency is closely linked to integrity. Integrity is the idea that the way I will behave in the future will be consistent with my character at present. It is only a common idea of what it means to be human that sustains integrity. For Butler there is no common humanity that we hold together and so integrity is up for grabs.

If we define our humanity according to strictly individualistic criteria, then there is no place for concepts of God, creation, revelation or sin. Absolutes are unacceptable. Rather than seeing sin as anything which transgresses God's moral boundaries and makes us guilty before him, we will see sin as anything that hinders my self-ctualization. Butler's argument places personal fulfilment over society and over holiness in an ultimate way. She is, in a real sense, an anti-Christ, in that what she teaches is not only anti-Christian, but so strongly anti-Christian that she defines Christian belief in God as immorality. This is surely perilously close to the unforgivable sin of blasphemy against the Holy Spirit, by taking the works of Jesus and attributing them to evil (see Mark 3:29). As part of this, heterosexuality is strongly attacked by Butler while any other expression of sexuality is strongly affirmed. She champions lesbianism as an alternative lifestyle that is at least as good as heterosexuality, and probably better.

Some responses to Butler

The Bible has a lot to say about who we are. It speaks of us being made in God's image, both male and female. We were made good but are fallen in every area due to our rebellion against God. We are, nevertheless, infinitely loved by him. He made us equal but different. Our difference is not a matter of status and we should never make it such. It is a matter of being made complementary. This complementarity extends to having different roles to play in God's creation. He made us, in fact, to rule over his creation. We are the highpoint of creation but remain under God's moral authority.

Our fallenness includes our sexuality and gender. It is no surprise that, following the fall, our sexuality is confused. This does not mean that God's gift of sexuality is bad or that his blueprint for its use is either inaccessible or oppressive. Rather, it means that we work best when we live God's way.

It is vital that we are secure in what God has said about us. If we are not, then we will be unable to test new ideas against God's blueprint for life. Each of the above points clearly denies Butler's position on sex and gender. In a world that rebels against God in its treatment of sex and gender, it is vital that we learn to live by standing firmly on biblical principles.

Christians must learn to understand what the Bible says – and then act on it

It is no good being hearers of God's Word only. Faith involves acting on what God says. This is a powerful apologetic for people taken in by the likes of Butler, because Christians can genuinely live better under God's blueprint than others can without him. How many times have you heard someone say that they first became intrigued with Christianity because of the quality of the life of a Christian? The likely outcome of Butler's writing is fragmented lives, sexual confusion and a poor sense of identity. Christians living authentically godly lives demonstrate that the gospel holds better answers. Of course, we are all the more likely to be persecuted as a result.

The New Feminist arguments are a good place to push conclusions to the logical extreme. Few people are a hundred per cent happy with paedophilia as an acceptable gender option. I grant that extreme cases don't prove the point, but they are good for raising the idea that there are other, better options.

We should recognize that the New Feminist arguments may contain a small grain of truth. In some ages men *have* oppressed women. While my personal feeling, having read Butler, is that the boot is now on the other foot, we should acknowledge the grains of truth when we find them. Christians must not oppress women. This means understanding from biblical principle what it means to have different roles and different identities. We must understand what it means for men and women to mutually submit to each other (Eph. 5:21), to support each other and work out our different roles in the church. So often the world has simply heard us saying, by implication, that all the important jobs, such as preaching, go to the men and all the menial jobs, such as cooking, go to the women. (To my mind it seems as if secular pressure against this unfair stereotype had a large influence on the issue of the ordination of women in the Anglican Church.) Regrettably, there is no room to explore gender roles in the church here, except to say that Christians must model good, biblical patterns, must not be misogynistic, and from Scripture must be able to clearly explain to outsiders what God thinks about men and women.

How does this affect our house-group member Sophie?

We have come a long way from our case study of a confused and hurting nurse. Some of the theory may not seem to immediately connect. Remember, however, that her interactive class strongly affirmed gender breakdown and the acceptability of homosexuality. It strongly refuted Sophie's desire to challenge homosexuality. By implication it challenged her own right to affirm her heterosexuality. The case study introduced the looming threat of further classes where this stance would be taught explicitly.

While Sophie may be only dimly aware of the full thrust of the theory, there is no doubt that it works powerfully in the lives of those in her class. There are likely to be three areas to her struggle.

The first is a social struggle. There are few things more painful than social rejection. It is hard to live what we believe when everyone else is enjoying immorality. Perhaps the most helpful thing for Sophie will be support from her church and house group. She needs encouragement from them to understand that, just as God wants her to grow in Christ-likeness and purity, so they wish to stand with her and help her. In the first instance she needs to know that

God forgives her for taking part in the class and then she needs to know that she has friends who wish to understand her situation and its particular struggles. Only with understanding friends and wise Christian leaders will she formulate a constructive and robust response in this hard situation.

In the second place, Sophie needs help to avoid moral compromise in her nursing situation. The pressure is on her from her contemporaries and from those who have the power to pass or fail her. Might it be better to withdraw than to remain in the place of temptation and pressure? It depends on the person. It would be very easy to place career above Christ in this situation and simply do what needs to be done in order to pass. It will be helpful if she has clear accountability with a trusted friend who will help her to maintain a strong witness and who will support her when she has to make tough decisions. The case study shows how anti-Christian theory results in deep anti-Christian pressure for Christians to act in ungodly ways. Careful pastoring is vital. How else should Sophie work out what it means to be Christian in her situation if not in the company of God's people?

In the third place, there are some things it would help Sophie to know in order to understand what lies behind some of the pressures in her nursing classes. Particularly, she needs to be aware of the inadequacy of arguments like Butler's, and where these arguments lead in the areas of sexuality and morality. She also needs to be familiar with a biblical position on identity, femininity and masculinity, to think about how we can see ourselves as God sees us, and to understand that living God's way makes us truly human as nothing else does.

Chapter 5
How Can We Know What Is Real?

The most radical end of Postmodern theory is now questioning whether we can actually know whether anything is real. After all, when we sweep away all foundations for knowing things or for making decisions, what is left? Among the most radical and famous commentators on culture is the French philosopher and literary theorist Jean Baudrillard (pronounced Bow-dree-ard). He started out as a Marxist critic but ended up as a pessimist who maintains that there is no longer any basis for critical theory. Or anything else, for that matter.

Baudrillard, however, is far from being written off for such pessimism. He is best known for playful, vigorous and provocative works of philosophy that, by his own admission, are as much about style of writing as they are about content. Much of Baudrillard's work exhibits a love-hate relationship with Postmodernism. He writes in ways that often pour scorn on contemporary Western culture, and yet he clearly enjoys producing relativist theory that denies value or truth. At one and the same time he tries to look beyond Postmodernism yet also makes a lot of money out of it.

Case study

Joy is a geography student. Bright and clever, she relishes the latest ideas. She also loves applying her faith to her study and tries to engage her culture whenever she gets the chance. One day Joy seeks you out with some of the hardest questions she has been faced with yet.

'I never expected to find so much cultural mumbo-jumbo doing a simple geography degree,' she said. 'But it seems that some trendy literary theorists have started talking about maps. They speak about "mapping reality". And the geographers kind of wanted to reclaim their territory (no pun intended), so they have started playing the philosophy game too.'

Literary theory and maps sound a bit odd to you, so you question further.

'Well, how would you respond to someone who says that our understanding of reality is like a map of reality, but that the real thing has somehow disappeared – that the map is the only thing left? And that we can't tell the difference between our map of understanding and what the reality was in the first place? I mean, that would just about destroy all foundations if it were true, wouldn't it? We just wouldn't know what was real in the world any more.'

It still sounds like a word game to you rather than serious geography, so Joy continues to explain: 'But the geography department is buying into it in a big way. They say that geography is now all relative to individuals and isn't based on any consensus. We all occupy our own spaces. Nobody else can understand the way I live in my space so it isn't really possible to do social geography any more. Everyone is coming to the conclusion that we are all so different that we are practically alone in the world.

'And as if that wasn't enough, they are saying that consumerism is producing mutated people. They say society is changing so fast that we will never be able to understand it, never be able to catch up with ourselves. It all boils down to people believing that it is now impossible to understand what is real.'

'But you don't believe that, Joy, do you?' you interject.

'No, no, I don't. But so many people are saying it that I am not sure that I can keep up with them intellectually. I feel like I am being swept off my feet, and to be honest there are times when I just don't know why I don't believe it. Everyone else seems so certain. I am hanging on with God, but I don't just want to do it blindly, any more than I want to follow the herd in the department blindly. I want to know if there are real answers that I can take back there.'

Some questions

Step back for a moment and consider some basic questions:

1. What sort of ideas is Joy being taught in the geography department?
2. Can you detect the underlying assumptions?
3. How could you begin to help her think through the academic issues?
4. What pastoral issues do you think are at stake here?

The theory bit: *Jean Baudrillard*

Books and movies

Lots of books and movies use the theme of a person who lives in a constructed world. Books like *Neuromancer* by William Gibson and films like *The Matrix* blur the boundaries between the real world and virtual reality. Perhaps the best recent example is the film *The Truman Show* – Truman lives in a totally artificial world. Yet from the inside he has been unable to tell the difference for most of his life. This sort of story is based on Baudrillard's theories.

One of Baudrillard's most famous comments is that we now live in a world that is not real but 'hyper-real'. What does this mean? The argument goes in several stages:

1. Once upon a time there was something called reality – the real world. It came to us unmediated, and we took it as we found it.
2. Then people started making maps of this real world. The maps are not the world but they tell you something about the world.
3. The modern media – films, papers, TV, the internet and other sorts of journalism – now begin to mediate the world to us in very powerful ways. It starts to become hard to work out whether what we are presented with is the real world or someone else's view of the world.
4. Finally this mediation through the media becomes complete. Baudrillard famously commented that we cannot possibly know whether the Gulf War actually occurred (he maintains, ironically, that it didn't!), because the *only* access we have to the facts is through TV – a medium which is utterly unverifiable by the public.
5. There is one further step, though. He also maintains that, in the case of the Gulf War, it was TV, the feedback of the media, the reaction of the public to carefully selected images, which controlled the actions and decisions of the military and political commanders. In other words they also cannot tell whether they are acting on the basis of the real unmediated facts, or someone else's version of the facts.

The world has become hyper-real for Baudrillard. Unmediated reality has disappeared, to be replaced by *simulation*. He uses other examples to make his point, such as flight simulators that are now so realistic that from within the system they are indistinguishable from actually being in a plane.

An important essay dealing with these issues is Baudrillard's 'The Precession of Simulacra'. It is well worth an hour's read, but let me summarize it.

The key points in 'The Precession of Simulacra'

Baudrillard maintains, first of all, that we live in a time where it is impossible to tell the difference between reality and simulation. We have no reference to God outside the system and no absolute standards. The breakdown between reality and simulation is complete because all external reference points are removed from us.

It follows from this lack of any outside reference point that there is no longer any discernible difference between truth and falsehood, reality and imagination. Baudrillard uses an example of a hypochondriac who produces his 'illness' so well that it is impossible to tell the difference between real illness and psychosomatic illness.

Furthermore, we cannot know God in this scheme of things because we cannot have any knowledge of the really real. Neither can we conceive of any communication that is not hyper-real. The only thing left to us, therefore, is simulation. 'Hyper-reality' is the *only* reality we can know, according to Baudrillard. Truth, reference and objectivity have ceased to exist.

Baudrillard goes ever further. This hyper-reality, he argues, is the only reality that *ever* existed at all – we never had access to truth, reference points or objectivity. If God cannot guarantee the difference between the real world and the false world, then there is no meaning, *nor has there ever been*! In Baudrillard's words, 'the whole system becomes weightless.' We have become just like virtual reality characters – a Truman or a Lara Croft.

Here is Baudrillard's own summary of his argument to this point:

> ***Baudrillard's summary***
> - An image reflects a basic reality.
> - An image masks and perverts a basic reality.
> - An image masks the *absence* of a basic reality.
> - An image bears no relation at all to any reality whatever. It is its own pure simulacrum.

Baudrillard's summary uses very religious language. He says that the result of his theory is that 'there is no longer any God to recognize his own, nor any last judgment to separate true from false, the real from its artificial resurrection, since everything is already dead and risen in advance.' At this point literary theory descends into pure blasphemy – a fact of which he is clearly aware.

That is Baudrillard's basic argument. There are a few more advanced steps he takes, but they are not essential for getting to grips with what he is saying.

We live in a world so thoroughly catalogued, he believes, that *all* our information and *all* our methods for processing information are now at least second-hand, and are affected by media spin. The problem is that nobody knows how much the ball is spinning, or in which direction. We are all lost. We cannot therefore speak about facts; we can only speak about different models of reality. No one model of reality is more valid than any other. Therefore our only option is to accept the situation and gracefully join in the simulation. Not even our personal identity is free from this. We *become* the simulation. The masks we wear do not cover up our selves – the masks are the only self we have.

He points out that the media that have created the spin

are dedicated to mass-consumerism. This consumerism, and the media that fuel it, is now inescapable. Everything and everyone, all ideologies and religions, indeed truth itself, have simply become products to be consumed. Truth is replaced by TV-truth, and TV-truth is all about the consumer as the centre of attention. Life is now indistinguishable from a film set; we are faced with 'the dissolution of TV into life, the dissolution of life into TV'.

More questions

At this point it is worth pausing to reflect on some fundamental questions:

1. Is any of this theory of reality and simulation relevant to Joy's geography classes? If so, how is it?
2. Is Baudrillard right or wrong? Why, in either case?
3. What can you affirm in the argument? What are the flaws in the argument?
4. How does his argument affect the way people think about the world?
5. Can you give some examples of where you have seen these ideas working out in practice?
6. How does his argument challenge a Christian understanding of (a) God? and (b) ourselves?

A Christian response to Baudrillard

Has life become TV?

We are fascinated by docu-dramas. TV and newspapers treat soap-opera events as though they are real. *Big Brother* reality TV claims to give us unmediated reality, but is pure simulation. The massive viewing figures show the huge popular attraction of Baudrillard's ideas.

Baudrillard is making powerful assertions about key foundations. He challenges the way we understand and approach reality itself. And we must deal seriously with his challenge, because plenty of people are listening to him. Here are a few thoughts about his ideas.

What is Baudrillard actually saying?

Baudrillard is very good indeed at rhetoric. Not that we should therefore write him off as being all style and no content, because with Baudrillard very often his style is his content. His medium is his message. But we should realize that he may not be saying the things he appears to be saying, but rather he may be trying provocatively to get people to think and approach the world in different ways. Baudrillard, for example, asserted loud and clear just before the event that the Gulf War would not happen. Following the war, he claimed that it hadn't happened. Was he therefore (a) ignorant, (b) suppressing the facts, (c) stupid, or (d) doing something different?

If we conclude that he was doing something different we start to see that the point of his work is not the same as its explicit message. In this case he was writing ironically, to get people to react to the media presentation of the war. He believed that merely writing another analytical article about the conflict would have little effect. Instead he wrote a sensationally provocative one with which absolutely everyone would disagree.

Why do I point this out? Because Christians need to engage with what contemporary thinkers are *really* doing. Their ostensible arguments might not be their actual point, as in this example. We must be seen to be understanding what is going on. A well-known theorist attacked Baudrillard for his writing about the Gulf War without understanding how he was writing. As a result that critic has himself suffered critical abuse. It can be similar with a Christian's response. One of the biggest barriers to being heard is that people simply believe us to be unthinking, unconcerned about issues that they consider important, and unwilling to spend the time investigating the issues.

Baudrillard and others like him are very slippery and clever writers. Unless we work at understanding them we will not only fail to hear what they are saying, but, critically, we will respond to things that they are not saying. Both failing to hear and hearing the wrong things will lose us hearers.

Understand the argument – examine the presuppositions

Because Baudrillard is very good with words and uses well-chosen examples, we can be blinded to the faults in the argument. The most obvious one from the article on simulation (and a very frequent one in much Postmodern writing) is that he presupposes his own conclusion and then sets out to demonstrate it. In the summary above, for example, you will see that the initial point in 'The Precession of Simulacra' contains a presupposition that there is no external reality and no absolute standards. There is no attempt to argue or demonstrate the point. In fairness we must concede that we now live in a world where most people assume that the point is self-evident. Nevertheless, it is a vital point to argue against because a great deal is built upon it.

How might we argue our contrary case? One possible way is to say that this sort of presupposing is exactly the thing that Postmodernists hate about much historical Christian argument. I know Christian students who have been attacked in class because the medieval Catholic Church stood on unchallengeable presuppositions – for example, refusing to believe that the earth orbits the sun simply because it goes against strongly received dogma. We would do well to point out that not only might the medieval Catholic Church not speak for all Christians, but also that Postmodernist presuppositions are often strongly received unchallengeable dogma.

Suppositions and presuppositions

One important matter to bear in mind when considering recent ideas about the world is that if we only ever discuss with non-Christians on the basis of supposition (i.e. a carefully developed argument), without also discussing on the level of world-view or presupposition (i.e. the foundations on which the argument rests), we may be blinded to the most glaring errors by any dazzling display of word-play.

Baudrillard's statements about God's absence and the weightlessness of the whole system rest on his own presuppositions. It is like saying 'God does not exist because I have pre-decided the matter.' All the argument does is try to ensure that the matter is no longer open for discussion. If we are able to deal at the level of presupposition, then we can make a good case for the fact that our presuppositions are, at the least, no more poorly attested than Baudrillard's. A relativist must recognize this level of presuppositions if they are to hold their position with integrity.

Check our own foundations

All Christians should be able to explain what we believe (1 Peter 3:15) and why we believe it. The benefits are obvious, but allow me to spell them out.

In the first place, by explaining like this we establish the credibility of the gospel before the world. It is not that we therefore rely on arguments rather than the Holy Spirit to convert people, but that we are concerned to demonstrate that the gospel is true and stands up to honest examination. Consequently our Christian lives are built on firm foundations and our witness is built on integrity and truth.

As we seek to build our lives on the firm foundation of God's Word and to develop powerful, credible witness, we can have no doubt that Postmodern theory is self-consciously trying to destroy all foundations, especially Christian ones. It is disturbing to find an increasing number of Christians who are converted, but even after months or years have little ability to explain even the most basic facts of the gospel, or to offer a reason for believing. 'I believe it because I do' is not an uncommon attitude. Previously, in a society that held some Judeo-Christian values, we could just about get away with that. Now we live in a society that is explicitly attacking Judeo-Christian values. Not only is it unacceptable to believe just because we do, it is positively dangerous. Blind belief is dangerous because it makes the gospel look like one not particularly credible option among many. And those who don't understand their own foundations are less likely to withstand any sustained challenge.

What, then, are our foundations? The Bible spells it out in lots of places. For example, we are told how we are to build our lives on God's revealed Word (2 Timothy 4). When we do so we stand firm. If we fail to do so we will fall down when pressures come. Jesus made exactly the same point when speaking of the two men building houses, one on the rock of the Word and the other on sand. Both houses looked good until troubles came and then the latter fell down. Of course, it is vital that we teach, train and encourage others in Bible understanding at all times, but even more so when we or Christians we know are facing the assaults of a hostile culture. After half a year of full-time study in Postmodernism my personal devotions were suffering badly. How grateful I would have been for mature Christian counsel, for help in understanding how the Bible provides a firm foundation, and for guidance in how to use the Bible to spot and challenge ungodly assumptions and arguments.

Compare biblical foundations with those presented by the world

The better we can vocalize the reasons why we believe things, the clearer the points of agreement and disagreement with non-Christian material stand out. You may find the following exercise helpful in this regard.

Exercise

Go back to the summary of Baudrillard's essay above (page 83). For each main point formulate a Christian understanding and response. Several issues arise straight away.

The first is that the argument is *based* on the idea of no external reference. We need to think about how to raise issues of creation, fall, revelation and omniscience. If God is real, personal, knows everything and speaks, then external standards are not in doubt. We can have confidence in the reliability of the message, because of the reliability of God's character and God's communication.

Secondly, we can recognize and applaud Baudrillard's honesty in taking his relativist argument to its ultimate conclusion – he has the courage of his convictions. Indeed if God is as far out of the picture as he says, then there is no other position to hold. But we can certainly ask the question, 'How does the argument stand up if God does in fact exist?' There is value in asking this question even to committed Postmodernists in a purely hypothetical way. It will demonstrate that while their position holds for them on their own terms, it needn't hold if those terms are wrong. Nor need it hold universal appeal.

In the third place, we should get used to asking searching questions. Postmodernists can be very dogmatic. There is no God and that is that. The trick is to ask questions that challenge presuppositions, but to ask them in unthreatening ways that will actually get people to think and answer constructively. The 'what if' way is a good starter. 'What if there was a God – how would that change the world? How would that change the theory? How would that change you?'

It follows, fifthly, that we can ask what difference it would make to the world and to ourselves if God does in fact guarantee the difference between good and evil, right and wrong, true and false, real and imaginary. It might even then be worth asking whether people think they would be better off under a Christian world-view than they are at present – purely hypothetical questions, of course!

By this point we have cast some doubt on presuppositions, hopefully encouraging people to look again at their foundations. They may even begin to realize that there is a credible alternative, provided they aren't locked into thinking purely in their own terms. By applauding Baudrillard's honesty we have affirmed something positive too. It is, of course, never good simply to be negative – it puts people off.

In the light of these issues arising from a Christian response and understanding, there are a few positive starting points I would choose that would help us to engage with Baudrillard's work. We can agree, for example, that we live in an image-conscious age. We can also agree that if God is not present then we have no absolute standards. We can agree too with his example of the hypochondriac. When we consciously build such bridges we are likely to earn a hearing. This was the way the Apostle Paul approached the academic culture of Athens in his own day (Acts 17).

Having gained a hearing, we are then in a position to start to raise questions. Helpful questions to raise with people who follow Baudrillard include the following: 'Do you really think that media manipulation is total? Are you really convinced that the triumph of image over content is universally true? Even in cultures with no TV? Isn't your view of media manipulation just forcing the whole world into a technological Western model of culture? Isn't that imperialistic? How can you say that the world is so thoroughly catalogued? Where is the evidence? Doesn't your total view imply transcendence – which is not possible on your terms?'

You get the idea. We have understood, listened, spotted the points of contact, and are now engaging. Few will be able to answer the questions above.

How does this help our student Joy?

It is a real pleasure to meet the occasional Joy. She doesn't want to simply regurgitate, but to think. Furthermore, she wants to think about her faith as much as her studies. The reason she is having difficulty is a good one – that she is committed to wrestling with hard issues. This needs to be pointed out to her. She needs to know that it is all right, even admirable, to struggle with such dilemmas.

Geography departments are certainly using this sort of theory to think about our perception of our world. We have seen, however, that the more important issue at stake is our understanding of foundations. A lot of the theory is vague, because it is based on style more than content. Hence there is plenty of room for Joy to ask in class: 'Just exactly what do you mean by that? What are the implications of what you are saying? On what foundations are your practices built?' Simply having some elaboration from lecturers about what they actually mean can be a great help!

Joy feels swept away in a tide of popular opinion. This sort of teaching is huge currency in universities. Lots of students buy into it because it feels like the cutting edge. There are good marks and funding money for those who enjoy these sorts of ideas. This means that the key task for anyone helping Joy is a pastoral one. Good friends and older Christians need to help her stand up as a Christian long enough for her to ask the pertinent questions. In my experience simply asking, 'Do you really believe this?' to a group of peers often got them to admit that they didn't, but that it was hard for them to go against the flow.

Joy needs to have the opportunity to (a) hear what is actually being said; (b) understand the argument and examine the presuppositions; (c) check her own foundations; (d) compare these with those from the theory; and (e) spot the right questions to ask in class.

This all takes time, during which she is vulnerable in a corrosive environment. She needs help during this stage of her life and study. Good Christian friends, lots of prayer for her, accountability with older Christians, a phone number of someone clued-up whom she can ring to chat to, are all possible lifelines. She needs help too to develop strategies for survival, then for engagement.

Part 2

CHALLENGING A CHANGING CULTURE

The writers and thinkers discussed in Part 1 are all self-consciously trying to 'think the future'. They desire to mould what life and belief will look like over the coming years. There seems little doubt that, barring the extraordinary work of God in revival, pluralist and relativist ideas will dominate our post-Christian Western culture. People will believe and tolerate nearly anything – as long as it isn't Christianity. Postmodernism is here to stay for the foreseeable future. While there are many who predict its downfall, I cannot agree with their confident expectations of something better to come. For Postmodernism is mainly about the rejection of authority and the enthronement of self. In the humorous words of one friend of mine, 'Postmodernism is a long, fancy word for sin.' Even were our cultural environment to change instantly and abruptly, the deification of self will remain the primary desire of our culture and society.

In Part 2 we shall consider how things have reached this current stage. Chapter 6 – 'The Changing Culture and the Postmodern University' – should be of interest to anyone who wants to understand cultural change in our day. The chapter deals quite extensively with the influential role of universities but is, I hope, useful for everyone rather than only students and academics. It is fairly demanding to read, so if you get bogged down, I suggest that you move on and come back to it later. Chapters 7 and 8 reflect on the dangers of allowing contemporary culture to creep into our Christian lives and our churches. Chapter 9 proposes that Postmodernism is not primarily a cultural phenomenon but a moral (or rather immoral) one, fuelled by the rejection of truth and maintained by the popular mass media, which are the subject of Chapter 10. Finally, the concluding chapter suggests ways to begin shaping our culture and arming ourselves for the cultural battles of a new century. Though shaped appropriately for our distinctive cultural context, the answers are, of course, the same as they have always been: to proclaim the unique Jesus Christ to the nations in the power of the Holy Spirit, with complete confidence that God will build his church and that the gates of hell will not prevail against it.

Chapter 6

The Changing Culture and the Postmodern University

People working in fields as diverse as classics, nursing, geography, theatre and the media have all recently told me that Postmodern ideas and values impinge on their work every day. At university Postmodern assumptions are often taught as truth, without their underlying assumptions ever being explored.

In this chapter we will look at how we have arrived at this Postmodern stage in our culture and, in particular, at the role that universities play in the equation. This chapter is especially useful for university students, their friends and those who pastor them. If you are going to university in the near future it will help you understand the culture you will find there. I hope, however, that even if you have no connection with further education, you will find the chapter a useful outline of where we, as contemporary people, have come from.

Where has Postmodernism come from?

The current Postmodern climate has a history which is worth knowing a bit about. It is largely the history of *how to represent reality*. We have always been fascinated with how to express the really real, whether it is through art, literature, philosophy, architecture or economics. To understand what is real and to be able to express it is a longstanding quest.

The Modernism that Postmodernism claims to come after is a phase in culture that is associated with the Industrial Revolution, with the triumph of reason and with a great surge in scientific discovery during what has become known as the European Enlightenment. The basic idea behind Modernism is that what is real is whatever is open to exact measurement by our senses. The goal of representing reality was understood as the ability to perfectly measure and convey an object, a place or a person. Perhaps the greatest popular Modernist hero is the *Star Trek* character Mr Spock, the Vulcan who sums up in his personality the triumph of reason and accurate measurement. He perfectly embodies the triumph of science. The invention of photography during the Modernist period was seen by many as the ultimate way to achieve this goal. Even Picasso could say that he had nothing else to learn about representation.

The failure to represent reality

Ironically, however, photography unwittingly started a crisis in representing reality. For while it does a pretty good job of recording an instant freeze-frame of a moment, it fails in many other areas which are crucial to understanding people and the world. It doesn't do a good job of capturing movement, a weakness that the Impressionists tried to correct in art. It replaces originality with technology. It only allows one viewpoint at a time. Through realizing the limitations of photography to capture and convey reality, our whole ability to precisely measure reality began to be called into question, and with it the Modernist quest for perfect, scientifically proveable data about what constitutes reality anyway.

Of course, this is a sweeping generalization for the cultural change of an entire generation. But photography really did challenge the idea of scientific representation of reality. In reaction Picasso and others started to paint their vision of reality in completely different and anti-representational ways – paintings of people with different numbers of eyes and noses in strange and impossible perspectives.

Similar things had already happened in philosophy, particularly with the work of Nietzsche. He is held in high esteem by many contemporary theorists, both for the philosophy he wrote and the way he wrote it. Nietzsche forged new paths by writing not in logical argument, but in pithy phrases, often unconnected, with the power of the soundbite rather than sustained debate.

In architecture the Modernist dream of efficient, clean lines and the organization of life by scientific principle was held in high regard in Nazi Germany and elsewhere. New materials allowed scientific concepts about the world and about ourselves to be shaped into structures in which to live and work. The last bastions of this idea are the crumbling 1960s geometric estates and tower blocks of the inner cities. Of course, the big problem with these constructions was that they were deeply inhuman and people found it nearly impossible to live in them. Small wonder that one influential Postmodernist, Charles Jencks, dates the end of Modernism to the moment when a particularly awful housing experiment in St Louis, Missouri – the Pruitt-Igoe housing scheme – was finally dynamited in July

1972, even though, when it was built, it was heralded as the ultimate expression of modern living.

The collapse of Modernism

There has been, then, a perceived failure to measure reality by a set of objective principles in any way that can actually be lived with. For example, Modernism heralded World War One as the war to end all wars – the war that would finally put an end to conflict, as we learned to put rational scientific principles into everyday practice. World War Two therefore raised a fatal challenge to scientific rationalism.

Philosophy

The development of thinking and philosophy over the Modernist period followed a parallel path. René Descartes was the great proto-Postmodernist. Everybody knows his famous phrase, 'I think, therefore I am.' Descartes was trying to find *in himself* some grounds for verifying knowledge without having to appeal to external authorities or to revelation. Initially this sort of thinking created the climate of self-confidence in which individualism and entrepreneurship led to the Industrial Revolution. But he also sowed the seeds of rampant fragmentation of society and ideas of truth. He moved his world from one in which objective truth could be known because it depended on God who reveals things truthfully, to one in which subjective knowers form from themselves and their experience the criteria of what may be known. Descartes replaced the idea that *God* knows everything and I will pursue *his* knowledge, with the idea that *I in myself* can know things without God and can pursue *my own* knowledge.

Some other thinkers

Several other thinkers added crucial elements to this basic idea. Immanuel Kant started to point out that we are not very reliable at knowing things. If all I can rely on is myself, that must mean that knowledge itself is increasingly inaccessible. Nietzsche added that it seems like nonsense to claim that there is a core kernel of truth, because we will never get to the point where there is nothing more that we can say about something. Jean François Lyotard summed it all up in his famous but confused book *The Postmodern Condition* with the assertion that we live in an age that is now characterized by 'a suspicion of metanarratives'. A metanarrative is a single overarching story, or explanation of reality, that claims to have all the answers. Christianity is an example, Modernism another, Islam a third and Marxism a fourth. The suspicion of metanarratives is the end of truth. We have moved beyond Mr Spock into *Star Trek: The Next Generation*, in which the science officer with his measurements is replaced by the empathetic Counselor Troi, and by Data, the android who wants to know what it is like to be human. A truthful understanding of the universe is no longer as important, it would seem, as a sensitive and subjective understanding of our inner selves.

A crisis of knowledge

Lyotard's statement is the natural outcome of the collapse of representation. He believes the Modernist ideas about measuring and categorizing reality are fatally flawed. We are now expected to accept that if overarching explanations of reality do not lead to humane living conditions, then the only alternative is to live by a set of micro-narratives. Each of us works out his or her own story, believing that any wider foundation for truth or behaviour is unavailable.

Many other thinkers have commented on this unavailability of knowledge. It is called 'the crisis of legitimation' by the philosopher Jurgen Habermas. The argument goes like this. There is no universal knower, no God to be accountable to. I am therefore the centre of everything. I must, however, decide the grounds on which I can know things. How do I decide what is true or false, right or wrong? To do so, I need further knowledge, which also needs to be verified by further knowledge, which also needs to be verified … and so *ad infinitum.*

Put simply, the theorists' claim is that *knowledge itself has collapsed under its own weight.* Postmodernists claim that knowledge cannot be verified. Therefore it is no longer possible to talk about facts or truth because, even if they exist, we cannot know them. Epistemology – the study of how we know things – is a dead and buried subject for most Postmodernists. It is simply not considered relevant any more. When Nietzsche – so important in all this thinking – said, 'God is dead', part of what he was saying was that we cannot base knowledge of God on any ground that we can know. And that renders God unknowable, doesn't it?

The deification of self

The final step in placing the self entirely at the centre of our framework for understanding reality is the contention that if there is no such thing as objective knowledge, then no significance can be placed on our actions or decisions or thoughts from without. There is no possibility that critical or value judgments can be verified by any external criterion. Hence the *only* available measure of significance, value or truth is the self. This is the ultimate end of the relativist position – that we are unable to know whether our values are good or bad. Indeed, the words 'good' and 'bad' no longer communicate anything of lasting significance, because they themselves do not relate to any external criteria for judgment, but mean only what the self wishes them to mean. As the novelist William Golding said, 'If God is dead; if man is the highest; good and evil are decided by majority vote.'

Cultural factors

The self is not a good arbiter of truth. We are altogether too selfish. What is now seen as good is whatever empowers the self or whatever meets my perceived needs. In today's culture what we perceive to be good *may* be near the truth, but it may not. In an individual world there is no way of knowing whether it is or not. Around this self we have created a narcissistic consumer society dedicated to pandering to perceived need.

There are many cultural factors that shore up the deity of self. Let me list a few.

1. The life of leisure

This culture of hedonism has drawn a sharp divide between public and private life. The private sphere is seen as what we really live for – the weekends. The private sphere is dominated by leisure activities, which are seen as the high-point of personal fulfilment. In which sphere has our Christian sub-culture established itself? The private. Hence it is automatically seen by the world as a leisure pursuit, and not something to intrude on the real world where decisions are made and everything of importance is decided.

In this environment there is a disintegration of work and play. We see work as a necessity and play as of real value. We work hard in order to enjoy our leisure. This distinction can mean that we lose the ability to apply our faith to our work or to our public obligations. At university it is common to find students who never think about their studies in the light of their faith, and equally common to find those who think harder about their studies than about their faith. It can seem better to be a thoughtful biologist or actor or English student than a thoughtful Christian. This sort of rigid compartmentalization between life and faith is very dangerous. It leads to academic and professional lives that have little Christian integrity and little powerful witness to the gospel. All this flows from believing that our Christian life is a leisure activity rather than the core of our identity. If we tread this path we fail to be salt and light in the world because we have no penetration of the world. The world will ignore us and we shall have brought it on ourselves.

2. Individualization

In a culture where most individuals have residual income to spend on luxuries, a vast machinery has grown up dedicated to the fulfilment of personal pleasure and the increase of personal choice. With no overarching values to be committed to, we substitute the fulfilment and marketing of self as the ultimate value.

Of course, in a Postmodern world there are no criteria for evaluating what is valuable and what is not. The result is that style is more important than substance in our society. The minute details of the lives of soap stars are given as much broadcast time as affairs of international importance. If there are no value markers apart from appearance and style, then presentation is the only thing left by which we can proclaim our worth. We naturally, therefore, define ourselves by the effort we put into our surface appearance – the clothes we wear, the places we visit, the company we keep. It is individualization that is responsible for the enormous growth in consumerism evident all around us.

In less technologically developed countries it is no surprise that there is less of an obsession with the cult of the individual. It is impossible to be obsessed with possessions without the technology to produce the products or to create the desire for them. In our culture, however, we define ourselves in terms of our technology – for example, reducing our relationships to email and the internet, thus destroying our communities; or, at the very least, we invent new definitions of community, as we live in one location, shop in another, socialize in a third and worship in a fourth. We now think about ourselves against a global backdrop that offers infinite possibilities for personal gratification. We believe sophisticated entertainment to be our right.

3. A delight in alternative culture

We live in a culture increasingly dedicated to the 'alternative' – the alternative lifestyle, the alternative comedian, so-called academic 'theories of alterity' and 'ethics of otherness'. If you want to know what is shaping contemporary culture, go and have a look at the culture books section in a Virgin Megastore, where an enormous range of alternative practices, sexualities, music and images vie for attention.

This is the fallout of rejection of authority. We would rather do anything than allow institutions to exercise authority. In the 2001 general election in Britain less than sixty per cent of the electorate turned out to vote, so disillusioned was the public with authority and public duty. If the church is an institution, then the thing to do is ignore it. If Christians claim historical precedents for truth, then ignore them too. 'Do your own thing, man' is the cry of a generation that believes that we make our own meaning now. But there are no anchors in the alternative world, no harbours for life's storms, because there is no authority and no authenticity. There is only style and image make-over, desperately trying to cover up the fact that at the heart of our culture there is nothing left of any value.

The universities

You may be wondering what all this has to do with universities. The answer is that universities produce the theory that undergirds rampant individualism. They also produce the books, the teachers and the personalities that continue the trends of Postmodernism. Universities delight in Postmodernism, which is seen as trendy and attracts a great deal of funding. This creates a slightly strange paradox. University research *produces* new cultural theories and artefacts – books, plays, ideas and strategies – and simultaneously *follows* current trends in order to remain financially viable. Thus universities both produce Postmodern culture and shore it up.

The assault on Christian truth is particularly potent in universities. Even in departments that are not obviously philosophical, like medicine or engineering, the values held by the students are often deeply relativistic and suspicious of truth. Days before writing this chapter I spoke to a number of geography students at a large and highly regarded British university. Without exception all told me that Postmodern ideas about truth affect their studies at all levels. 'Geography today,' they told me, 'is concerned with remaking the world as we would like it to be – and that can be whatever we want.'

In the everyday world we see the outworking of relativism and pluralism in consumerism and individualism. Day to day, however, we do not generally experience the academic foundations on which our culture rests. But in universities, we discover not only the outworking but the foundations as well. Here is a situation where the theory and the culture produced by the theory have a very strong mutual interest in maintaining and upholding each other.

There are several consequences of this symbiosis. The first is that universities are potent producers of culture in

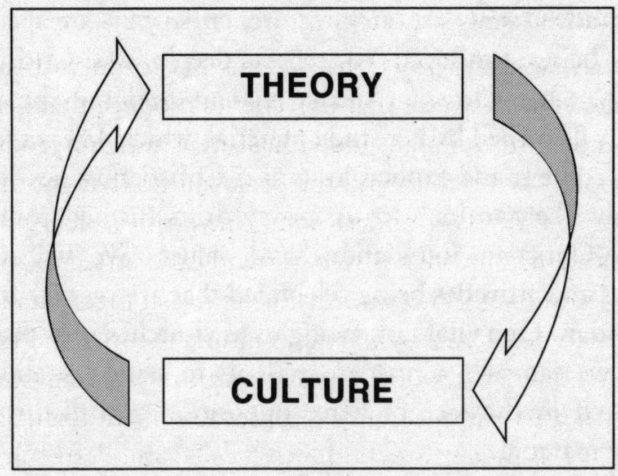

their own right. Many contemporary novels now have cultural theory writ large on every page, if only we know how to read the signals. Umberto Eco, Thomas Pynchon, Angela Carter and William Gibson, to name but four writers, all use the theme of unknowability.

A second consequence is that universities will continue to produce and uphold this sort of culture through the graduates they produce. This year's undergraduates are next year's journalists and TV producers. The values they pick up from their theoretical framework will dramatically affect the diet of news and entertainment that we will receive in the coming years. By 2010 one half of British young people aged between eighteen and twenty-one will be in some form of tertiary education. This is social engineering on a massive scale. Universities present big opportunities for the gospel, but opportunities that we shall only begin to seize when we understand the culture that students find themselves in, the content of the material that they are taught and the struggles and challenges faced by the Christian students who find themselves at university as Christ's ambassadors.

A third consequence is that cultural artefacts – books, films, advertising, art, architecture, criticism – are specifically being produced to reflect deeply anti-Christian theory. One Christian media student told me she was deeply disturbed by her study material, which was perverse in its content and explicit in its anti-Christian values. This is only likely to increase as society drifts further from its Judeo-Christian foundations and values. We will find values and attitudes being celebrated that are very far from Christian. One vital task facing us as churches is to decide how we can help Christian students to stand up and be counted in the face of fierce opposition and disturbing study material.

A fourth result is that reaching universities with the gospel is hard because of the strong mutual support of theory and culture. It is vital that we do so, however, and that we do so by hitting not just the theory or just the culture, but both. It is not enough simply to do good academic work without speaking to the culture at large, or vice versa.

Universities and Postmodern theory

We looked in depth at specific theories in Part 1. It is worth noting that universities are the places where this far-reaching theory is produced and circulated. This is especially true of English Studies, but also of Drama, Film, any kind of Cultural Studies, Philosophy, History, Politics and Economics, Geography, Sociology, Languages and Psychology.

English is a particular breeding ground for Postmodern theory, because of the sheer amount of time and effort being expended in writing on the two subjects of *Discourse* and *Language*. Why are these two areas so important?

It is argued that the collapse of Modernism has shown that objective reality is not representable. Indeed, it is not actually accessible because all ideas or approaches to the world come through subjective people. 'Even if there is objective reality,' argues the Postmodernist, 'subjective people cannot access it or communicate it.' Even if truth does exist, it exists in an *X Files*, inaccessible, 'out there' sort of way.

The question is then asked: 'How *do* we access the world?' Much contemporary theory teaches that the world is *only* available to us through language. The claim is made that, without language, we are unable to think. Hence both thinking itself and our access to the world around us are merely constructed out of the language we use.

All of a sudden the whole world has been defined as a *text* – something with a story. For the Postmodernist we bring the meaning to the story ourselves. The theory suggests that we can deal with the world and everything in it, including ourselves, as a text or discourse for analysis.

From here all sorts of other results follow. Here are a few of them.

1. We cannot discover meaning in the world

Because we all approach the world via our own micro-narratives, and have no criteria for judging our stories to be better or more true than anybody else's, then similarly we have no criteria for giving meaning to anything in the world other than purely personal preference. Just as a reader, it is claimed, brings meaning to a book, so we bring meaning to the world. There are, however, as many different meanings as there are different people, and all are equally valid.

2. We can deconstruct the world

The tools that literary theorists use to examine books are equally valid with the whole world if the world is considered to be a text. This is most notably true of deconstruction.

As we have seen, deconstruction leaves the self as the only arbiter of right and wrong. But the self isn't very good at it. Theorists are keen to see the self as a text, or better yet a collection of texts that all say different and contradictory things. This, they claim, is why we are not good at deciding on knowledge, because our internal communication is incoherent. Not only can we not communicate with others as they speak 'different vocabularies' to us, but ultimately we cannot communicate with ourselves either. All that is left is inner turmoil. This, too, is an argument taken from study of more conventional texts.

3. We must be politically correct

Deconstruction tries to show that a text has an underlying agenda or power claim. For example, it is suggested that history is always written by the winners. Therefore to re-enfranchise marginalized groups, we should re-read the winners' texts of history (usually disparagingly) in a way that will positively discriminate in favour of the perceived losers. Apply this principle to politics or to reasonable debate, and most arguments can be happily dismissed or written off as a power game if we disagree with them. The result is a 'political correctness' that holds it to be deeply inappropriate to challenge the position of anyone else, whilst highly appropriate to re-read any text according to our own agenda. After all, if the author's intent is either unknowable or suspect, then the best use we can make of any text is for it to serve our own ends. This is, of course, a power play that is just as manipulative as any of which marginalized groups accuse others.

Anthony Thiselton helpfully confronts this tendency to re-read texts through an agenda. He says that such re-readings remove anything from the text that does not affirm the hopes and aspirations of the group who are doing the reading. As a result, he says, such re-reading can never truly be liberating. For rather than speaking freeing truth to the group, the text merely becomes imprisoned within the priorities and aspirations of the group – it only ever says what the group want it to say. A text thus becomes an ideological tool, but one that is fatally flawed because the group cannot distinguish its own perspectives from the perspectives of the text.

Thiselton concludes: 'Any merely selective use of texts to encourage those who are oppressed [or who maintain that they are oppressed, which can be a very different thing] can be perceived in principle to represent precisely the same strategy of hermeneutical method as the oppressors who use texts to legitimise their own programmes.'[1]

In other words, political correctness makes precisely the same mistakes that it accuses others of, and uses exactly the same tools of oppression to try to stifle other voices.

4. There is no centre to life

If we only experience the world through micro-narratives, even the self we place so much trust in is unimportant. The self is (to use the technical phrase) *decentred*, shifted to the periphery of meaning rather than the centre. The trouble is that there *is* no other centre. Meaning is rendered completely unattainable, even in a subjective, personal sense.

Conclusion

All these theoretical pronouncements arise from university departments. In many cases the cultural outworking of them is clear to see in social fragmentation, political correctness, relativistic thinking, philosophical (and in some cases Christian) pluralism, the lack of confidence in the text of Scripture to communicate meaning, and the lack of confidence of Christian university students to challenge their friends, let alone their lecturers.

The situation has been a long time coming. Its foundations are far from neutral, spiritually speaking. Eastern religious thought heavily influenced much of Nietzsche's philosophy. It is no surprise that New Age thinking is one product of relativistic pluralism. The project to write off Modernism, while perfectly valid in many ways, was also a project to write off the idea of revelation, objective truth, and God, often explicitly so. As a race we continue to turn our backs on him.

In our day, and in our universities, we see many factors combining to produce theory and culture that firstly make the human being king over all, and then dethrone the human being, leaving nothing at all in its place. While contemporary theorists claim not to be nihilistic about meaning, truth and the world, but rather to be playing with ideas and 'thinking the future', it is hard to ignore the wag who described Postmodernism as 'nihilism with a grin'.

Both culture and theory come together in universities to produce a potent cocktail which heavily influences all of life, even outside of education. We are seeing the rise of a generation of young thinkers with presuppositions utterly opposed to the gospel. At the same time the environment is becoming increasingly caustic for Christian students who are faced with the need to engage with university life at both academic and social levels, but are often ill equipped to do so.

Some questions

1. If you are a student, are you aware of challenges to the gospel and your Christian life from Postmodernism in your place of study?
2. How do you respond?
3. If you know students, are you aware of the sorts of challenges they face being Christians at college?

4. Ask some of them how you can pray for them and support them more effectively.

Chapter 7

Postmodern Christian Living 1: Postmodern Bible Reading?

Postmodern*ity* describes the cultural setting in which we live in the West at the start of the twenty-first century, with all its innovations in technology and media. Postmodern*ism*, however, is a value system which renounces authority. It is the outworking of Lyotard's 'suspicion of metanarratives'. This suspicion is levelled at all authority structures but is most strongly targeted at institutions that, it is claimed, have historically disenfranchised and marginalized minority groups and silenced dissent. The church – and by extension Christianity – is held up as a prime example.

I do not want to debate here the rights and wrongs of who has done what to whom over the 2,000 years of Christian history. It is, however, important to see that many associate Christianity with oppression and marginalization by appealing to events that may have no relation to biblical Christianity at all (and may even have been abuses of religion masquerading as Christianity). By this sleight of hand the Postmodernist will happily write off the Christian with no reference to what they believe, but simply according to how they think some Christians *may* have behaved. This is not to say that Christians exist in sinless superiority and never act poorly, but simply that Christian claims for the truth of the gospel are often not even up for discussion.

This is, of course, very convenient if the very thing you wish to avoid is any claim to truth. It is much easier to write off Christians on other grounds than to have to discuss Jesus and whether there is good evidence for God revealing himself authoritatively in his Word. Ever since Nietzsche the most well-worn strategy has been to label any truth claim as a 'will to power'. It is widely held that any claim to power is bad, and any truth claim is a power play. Thus truth claims are immoral and oppressive from the start. How could it be otherwise in a world where self is the only arbiter of value and meaning? For in that world there is neither transcendent truth nor any meaning that is not established by reference to individual people. There are no reference points. God is dead.

The flip side of the coin is that while Postmodernists don't like to talk about the depth and substance that Christians claim for the gospel, the system they advance in its place is deliberately shallow and superficial. Postmodernism is playful on issues of truth and disparaging and sarcastic about those who think otherwise, without ever listening to them. It is pragmatic about what makes us human. It is selfish about the primacy of the individual as the arbiter of truth and conduct. It is destructive of any social behaviour based on any virtues that are larger than the individual, such as promises or integrity, opting instead for the pragmatic 'Does it work for me?'

These two strategies – silencing Christians' claims to

truth without listening to them, and setting up alternative ways to live that are unconcerned about truth issues – have one major effect on all of us: that we are now suspicious of things that claim to be true, simply on the grounds that they claim it! It has become the automatic response of a culture to junk truth without ever asking if we do so for substantial reasons or merely pragmatic ones. The assumption is either that there is no such thing as truth, or, if there is, it is unknowable or plural.

Some questions

Pause for a moment to ask yourself some basic questions:

1. What is truth?
2. Where does truth come from?
3. How is truth knowable?

The suspicion of truth is as likely to affect Christians as non-Christians. After all, we all live in a culture that bombards us with messages to this effect. It is not surprising to find Christians who have either never been sensitized to think about whether things are true, or who have been worn down by the continual war of attrition waged by the media. The effect on our devotional, personal and church lives can be enormous.

Postmodern Bible reading?

One Christian student said to me, 'Surely if the Bible says one thing and I strongly feel another, the only thing I really have to go on is my feelings.' In other words, while converted, she no longer had any confidence that reliable access to truth was available in the Bible, or indeed anywhere. Feelings were, for her, the most trustworthy thing to go on. Another example we meet with alarming frequency is the idea that any Bible passage speaks directly to me, without reference at all to its original meaning. The Bible can say what I want it to say. What it meant to the person who wrote it and to those for whom it was originally written is often treated as irrelevant.

Applying the Bible badly

In a recent Bible study training session I suggested to a group that before we can ask 'What does this passage mean to me?' we must ask 'What did it mean to the original recipients?' This alone caused enough difficulty for the group, who would use every example of the word 'you' in Scripture as a direct reference to them as individuals (in the positive cases anyway, or where blessing is promised rather than curses!). But when challenged with a passage that absolutely could not be directly describing them, one member of the group replied along the lines of 'I can see that this passage means one thing when set in its context, but the Holy Spirit is also interpreting it to me now to mean something quite different.' When asked if the Holy Spirit uses the same text to mean contradictory things depending on how the reader wants to see it, and whether this doesn't make the Holy Spirit schizophrenic, the person replied, 'Well, yes, I suppose that is what I think.' He was a pluralist – converted, almost certainly – but powerfully influenced by the world's ideas about truth.

Similarly, in a recent Bible study I attended, a group member suggested that a verse meant something that it clearly didn't. When the leader gently questioned his understanding of the verse, he responded, 'But that's what my experience tells me.' The group leader, unsure what to do, diplomatically decided to move to the next question, leaving the tension unresolved. But here is the worrying thing – the person's experience was the *only* evidence produced to make up his mind about what the Bible says. There was no thought that the Bible then changes its meaning if you have a different experience, still less that it is necessary to know what a passage originally meant and how *that* might apply today. Yet again, feeling, not truth, was the arbiter of what God was saying.

This, of course, will not do! At best it shows that many misunderstand the relationship between the Holy Spirit and Scripture. 'The Spirit inspired Scripture,' the argument goes, 'and the Spirit lives in me. So any internal prompting I sense when reading the Bible is the Spirit illuminating the text.' At worst, there is little idea at all that the Bible is God speaking and Scripture is reduced to a collection of wise sayings from which to pick and choose. Either way, we come very close to believing the Bible can mean just what I would like it to mean.

The Bible and authority

What underlies these sorts of common misconceptions about the Bible? It is not just that we are losing our ability to think clearly about the Bible, about how we should expect it to work and how we should approach reading it or listening to it. More fundamentally, we are losing our ability to think *evangelically* about the Bible. That is, we listen to sermons and attend Bible studies, but without basic convictions about what the Bible actually *is*.

This is a major factor in the way that Evangelicalism is fragmenting. There is surely scope in Scripture for biblical Christians to disagree amicably over secondary issues such as baptism or the specifics of church membership, whilst holding a common understanding of what Scripture actually is. The desire in any such disagreement is always to establish what the Bible really says in order that we may obey it. It is not a matter of questioning what the Bible is – the very Word of God written. On that matter there is a deeper unity that holds people together through many more minor disagreements.

When we treat the Bible as a mere guidebook or manual for living, however, the fundamental ground for agreement between believers disappears. If it is just a random collection of profound thoughts from which to cherry-pick our favourites, or a guru to whom we can bring all our most searching questions, then what we feel the Bible says to us personally is more important than working together to reach agreement (however hard) over what God has actually said. In this second case we have become Christian pluralists, and that is unacceptable.

The failure of this approach is that it asks, 'What can I do with the Bible?' This is the wrong question. It assumes that the Bible is there primarily to answer my questions, for me to decide what bits are relevant to me, for me to take the bits I like or think I understand. I am in the centre. Rather than sitting *under* God's Word and admitting that it has authority over me, I sit in judgment *on* God's Word and assume that my needs and desires are authoritative over it. This is simply Postmodern individualism with a Christian gloss. It is, perhaps, the subtlest way we see Postmodern assumptions creeping into our lives and the church. Most dangerously, it assumes that I am the one who can best decide what is relevant to me and that it is fine for me to read the Bible selectively on that basis. Yet if we accept that the Bible is the very Word of God, then nothing could be further from the case. It is not I but God in his Word who decides what is most relevant for me to know. I have no freedom to read or apply it selectively, because it is all relevant.

While we continue to approach the Bible in this way, we refuse to accept God's revelation of himself on his own terms. Therefore we don't accept God's revelation of himself at all. We fail to grasp what Scripture actually is. There is one God, with one plan of salvation through the one man Jesus Christ, that he tells us about in one book and illuminates by one Spirit.

We meet misunderstandings over Scripture in the most unlikely places. It is not, as many conservative churches would like to think, something that is merely limited to less conservative fellowships and denominations. There are many churches that pride themselves on being 'Reformed', who say they place a high premium on preaching, but in which the same four-point gospel message is preached every week, regardless of the Bible passage under examination. This is just as bad a model of how to handle Scripture as the church that places the authority of Scripture on a par with contemporary prophecy. Neither really takes the Bible seriously on its own terms, neither sits under Scripture's authority, neither has a firm grasp on what the Bible actually is.

Pause for a moment and honestly ask yourself whose authority you sit under when you study the Bible? Is it the Bible's or is it your own? Do you come asking God to speak about matters that he thinks are important, or do you cherry-pick favourite bits and ignore the rest? What about in church on Sunday? Under whose authority do you sit there? Is the Bible taught with a view to really exposing you to what a passage says, or does the minister provide the same sermon with a different spin week after week? If the latter, then you must ask, 'Are we sitting under the authority of the Bible or the authority of our minister?'

What is the Bible?

Postmodernism rejects authority. People want to get to the end of their lives, hold their head high and sing, in the words of Frank Sinatra, 'I did it my way.' Everything in Western society and culture is dedicated to achieving this vision. But the Bible cuts right across the popular assumption.

Scripture claims that the desire for total autonomy and self-reliance is at the heart of rebellion against God. We were not made to be autonomous; we were made for his glory and to enjoy a Father-child relationship with him. The desire for self-actualization that stands at the heart of relativism and philosophical pluralism must make any Bible-believing Christian very uneasy. Christians want to know not how great we are, but how great God is. What is important is not what we think, but what he thinks. And then we want to submit ourselves to his will, because his desires for us, and his care of us, are better than we can hope to achieve for ourselves. When we submit to God in joyful obedience, not only is he glorified, but we are satisfied. When we enjoy and obey him, then we are most fully human.

The Bible claims to be the very words of God. It claims to be God-breathed or God-exhaled (2 Timothy 3:16). To be a bit provocative, this means that it is quite hard to separate the Bible from God! We must never become bibliolaters – Bible-worshippers – but we must recognize that it is as impossible to separate God from his Word as it is to separate my words from me. Only more so, because God's Word enacts God's will perfectly in a way that my word does not. God's Word comes by the breath of God's Spirit, and is effective and acting. We should be very careful before we separate God from his Word or God's Spirit from the Word.

God's Word is active and effective because it is the sword of the Holy Spirit. It is the Spirit's offensive weapon to fulfil the purposes of God both in us, and in the heavenly places (Ephesians 6:17). It is authoritative over us because God's person guarantees God's Word. Which, incidentally, is the reason why Scripture is without error. God's Word can no more be inconsistent or wrong than can his character or person. If we believe that Scripture contains errors, we believe some shaky things about God himself. As Wayne Grudem puts it, all the words in Scripture are

God's words in such a way that 'To disbelieve or disobey any [word of Scripture] is to disbelieve or disobey God.'[2] And that is sin.

What does the Word do?

But what is God's Word active and effective to do? We could list many things. Here are just three from one small part of John's Gospel: we are *clean* because of the Word spoken to us (15:3); disciples of Jesus are *sanctified* by the Word (17:17); Jesus prays for those who will *believe* through the message (17:20), and those who believe have life (as 20:30–31 tells us).

We are clean not because of some contemporary word, but because of *that* Word that Jesus spoke to the disciples. He is still speaking it. He has not changed it; he isn't saying something else or telling some other way to be clean. We aren't sanctified by a new prophecy but by *that* Word. We don't believe and have life through a brand-new word; we have life through an *eternal* Word. Jesus, in person, was the way the disciples got to know God and had eternal life. Jesus, in person, is the way we get to know God and receive eternal life, through the message, by the power of the Holy Spirit.

I hope you see why this is important. We don't receive the blessings we hear about in John's Gospel, and many other places, without the eternal Word of God. We don't get to know God without the Word. We may know he is there but we cannot have saving knowledge of him. Otherwise it would be possible for people to be saved without the gospel.

At the very least, then, the Bible is trustworthy and reliable (or inerrant and infallible, if you want the theological terms) because it is grounded completely in God's consistent character and his ability to communicate truly and successfully. It is, furthermore, our source of truth *about*

God. The Word is God's appointed method of communicating to the world. It is God's self-disclosure through his actions in history and his own explanation of those actions. The Bible is also the bedrock of our relationship *with* God, because the Holy Spirit is at work when we hear and obey it. The Bible in fact provides the big picture of God's unfolding purposes to undo the effects of sin and restore sinful people to himself through the cross of Jesus Christ. It is important to underline that the Bible is much more about God than it is about me. It represents what God thinks is relevant for us to hear, regardless of what we think is relevant. Indeed, we can only discover whether our concerns are relevant or not when we evaluate them beside God's concerns.

Because Scripture is all this, Paul can tell Timothy (2 Timothy 3:15–17) that it is essential for salvation; that it teaches us (enabling us to know and understand God); that it rebukes us (when we ignore or disobey God); that it corrects us (setting us on the right track); and that it trains us in righteousness (it is our textbook for holiness).

Bible-believing Christians have the conviction that the Bible is God telling us about himself and about how we can know him and relate correctly to him. It tells us what our attitude should be towards him: wise and obedient. It tells us how to respond to God and gives us proper understanding. It teaches us how to be equipped for God's work. Our growth and the growth of our churches depend on it. That is why evangelical Christians have always held the Word of God to be central. We are first and foremost Bible people, concerned to be biblical in all we do.

Reading with Postmodern spectacles

What happens, however, if I read the Bible through Postmodern spectacles? What are the implications if I read it asking merely, 'How can the Bible seem relevant to me?'

or 'How can I use the bits I like to say the things I like?' The above points about the nature and trustworthiness of Scripture are turned on their heads.

In the first place, it doesn't matter whether the Bible is reliable and trustworthy, because the important thing is not to hear what God is actually saying, but to take the bits I like and apply them to myself. So when I come to the Bible, what I find there is not revelation, but wish fulfilment.

The Bible, furthermore, is not the source of truth about God, because I read it selectively. This betrays a casual disregard of what God says about himself. Rather, I look to the Bible to find subjective statements about myself. I also tend to edit out the parts that are tough to understand or that say things I may not like to hear.

In the third place, the Bible is no longer the bedrock of my relationship with God. It does not tell me about him on his own terms. Nor do I recognize the role of the Spirit in taking the real things of God and applying them to my life. The Bible is a text for me to use for my own purposes rather than my way to submit to the Spirit's teaching, correcting, rebuking and training in righteousness. I fail to understand Scripture or take seriously the fact that the Bible is Spirit-breathed.

Fourthly, the Bible does not give me the big picture of God's work in his world. (The big picture is irrelevant because it is a metanarrative.) What matters is not God's great dealings with his people and his grand plan of salvation, but my experience in the present.

In the fifth place, the Bible tells me much more about me than about God. I go to it to find lessons about me rather than about him. The application of every sermon I hear should be something about me or something for me to do, rather than something about God that makes me stand in awe of him.

Finally, the parts of the Bible I don't understand I can

consider to be irrelevant to me. Even more irrelevant to me are the bits I think I understand but the implications of which I don't like!

We all stand in danger of the subtle blandishments of Postmodernism. The idea that we can make the Bible mean what we would like is deeply popular. The idea that we might have to apply ourselves to the hard work of studying it is not. But this is just laziness, and dangerous laziness at that. Do we not think God's Word is worth some effort? Have we not understood that the Spirit uses the Word to make and shape God's people? If we are unconvinced about truth, then we shall certainly not take care to use our Bibles well. This means that we will not hear God speak and that we shall lose any confidence that the Bible is the Holy Spirit speaking to us now.

We see the effects of this all over the place. There is no question that this generation has a huge interest in 'spirituality'. Bookshops devote many shelves to 'body, mind and spirit' sections. Selections held together by nothing more than the fact that the books in them seem to be about spirituality. The books may cover things as different as dieting and astrology, medieval English churches and Zen, but that doesn't matter in the body, mind and spirit section.

This section in your local bookshop has become, in itself, a remarkable demonstration of what happens when Postmodernism encounters the world of religion. The overall emphasis is one of totally subjective engagement with myself. Some notion of God or spiritual forces may get a look in for the sake of personal spiritual enrichment or guidance. What is noticeably lacking in the body, mind and spirit section is anything at all on enrichment and guidance through obedience to the Word.

Tragically, many Christian bookshops are not much better. The bookshelves of many Christians are filled with volumes that don't give us any confidence in the Bible. It should come as no surprise, therefore, when we find Christians who neither live by the Bible nor even know why they should. The Bible is eroded and the result is drift. The unspoken belief of many is that the Bible is for purely private interpretation and can mean something different to everybody. What matters is whether I get a buzz out of reading it. I would go further and say that another result of relativism slipping into the church and our Bible reading habits is apathy. People eventually realize that the subjective buzz doesn't satisfy because they don't really hear God speak at all. The end point is that many stop reading the Bible altogether. We end up with impoverished discipleship and mission that has nothing concrete to offer to a world in need.

Regaining lost ground

Before I offer some suggestions on how to confront the effects of Postmodern Bible reading, I would ask you to pause and consider the following questions, questions I have had to ask of myself:

1. How is your own personal Bible reading going? Is it regular, stimulating and satisfying or patchy, heavy and dull? Do you come to the Bible determined to discover what God thinks or to affirm what you think?
2. What factors underlie your answers to question 1?
3. What is the Bible? Why should you read it?
4. What regular sources of input do you have to help you with the Bible (e.g. sermons, Bible study groups, reading it with someone else, using notes, commentaries or tapes)?
5. Can you describe your own growth in Bible understanding over the last year? If not, have you perhaps moved backwards?

6. What is the quality of Sunday sermons in your church like? I don't mean are they entertaining and easy to listen to, but do they really get you to look at the Bible? If not, why not?
7. Do you currently have an appropriate attitude towards the Bible as God's very words written? If not, what steps do you need to take to put this right?
8. Does your Bible reading give you Christian confidence and joy?

There are many reasons why our Bible stays closed on the shelf. The assumptions of the culture around us may not be the only cause of a dusty Bible, but they certainly discourage us from getting to grips with it. The world offers more amusing and instantly stimulating alternatives.

Having a closed Bible is the best way to slide backwards in the Christian life. Maybe we make a deliberate decision, a bit like teenage rebellion; maybe other pressures crowd in on us and make us neglect our walk with God; maybe we are simply careless and forget that all relationships need feeding and sustaining, most of all our relationship with our heavenly Father. For whatever reason, it is possible to neglect the Bible and go backwards instead of forwards. In fact if we are not going forwards we are probably going backwards by default. There is no place in the Christian life for coasting along in neutral. It is either one or the other. The Postmodern world has a large interest in making us drift in our Christian lives.

I don't know of any Christian who never has dry times. The Bible sits on the shelf and we think, 'I haven't spent any time reading it lately – maybe tomorrow.' My intention is not to batter you, making you feel guilty about not reading your Bible. It is not a sin not to read your Bible every day, and feeling bad isn't going to help you read it any more. But I do want to encourage you that it is a very good thing to do.

Bible convictions

Unless our convictions are set straight we will not be convinced that the Bible is worth persevering with. Of course, there are consequences if we do not read the Bible. We can try and search out God but we can never know if what we have found is reality. We can try to live wisely but we cannot know if our lifestyle is in line with God's character and wishes. We can try to please him, but we are doing it on our terms, not his. We can try to find satisfaction in other things, but only God really delights us eternally. We can try to live by grace, but we are likely to live by other things, because only the true God provides living water for our souls. His self-revelation by the Holy Spirit, through the Word, is satisfying for our spirits – refreshing, revitalizing, cleansing, sanctifying, holy truth.

Practical help

How does the Bible actually work? How does reading it and hearing God speak actually make a difference? Psalm 119, the longest psalm, is a great poem about living as a biblical Christian. It is a clever acrostic, written so that every stanza starts with a different letter of the Hebrew alphabet. In other words, the writer is presenting an A-Z of living God's way.

Psalm 119

Spend a few minutes reading the first four sections of Psalm 119 (verses 1–32). Then consider the following questions about each section (1–8, 9–16, 17–24, 25–32):

1. What areas of a Christian's life are impacted by God's Word?
2. What should we do with God's Word if we want it to have an effect?
3. What happens if we don't delight in God's Word?
4. Why does the Psalmist feel the way he does about God's Word?

Psalm 119 tells us that the way to live a godly life is to live according to God's Word. This is the way to discover the blessing of a blameless walk and the means to keep our way pure. But it tells us more than this. It tells us we are strangers here on earth (verse 19). Living by the Word is the successful way to live as a stranger, looking forward to what God has planned for us in heaven. The psalm tells us how we should live when arrogant people hate us for belonging to God. It tells us what to do when we feel like we are at the bottom of a pit. It tells us where to find strength when we are weary, and the ability to do right when we are tempted to be deceitful. In short, it is the way righteous people learn to be equipped for every good work.

Can you see why the Psalmist finds delight in God's Word? It is his joy, his food. He is consumed with longing for the words of God. Are you consumed with longing? When you open the Bible don't do it casually; you are going to hear God speak!

Let us be realistic. We know we should love reading the Bible more than we do. But it is hard sometimes. Often we don't have good Bible study habits. We struggle with how to apply it to ourselves, and maybe settle for the bits we like. And, of course, our sinfulness makes us want to disobey. The Devil is never happier than when our Bibles are closed. He doesn't want us to have delight in our God, and he gladly puts distractions in our way.

So how can we practically make sure that we are soaking ourselves in the Bible? At the end of the day, this is the only solution to the Postmodern suspicion of truth and dismissal of authority. Here are a few ideas that I have found helpful. Perhaps you could take one or two and try them out this week.

First of all, good Bible study patterns don't just happen. They need to be learnt like any other skill. Just like any relationship, this one needs an investment of time. Have a regular time and place to read the Bible. Be disciplined. Don't seek God in a shoddy way. Be aware of the inertia that comes when we don't believe Bible truth but instead soak up the assumptions of the age that everything is here to please us.

Secondly, why not find someone with whom to read the Bible? It need not be frequently, but it will help you if you do so regularly. I would recommend once a fortnight, but if this is too much, then why not once a month? The time commitment is a small price to pay for the benefit of having another person who will encourage you, and who you, in turn, can spur on.

Thirdly, read large chunks of the Bible. Don't settle for a few nice verses. Go for a book. Read it over a week or a month and find out the whole message of the book. It is meant to be read like this, not in little pieces. Be systematic. The mark of Postmodern Bible reading is the person who goes to the Bible for instant gratification, or who expects to open it at any random page and take the first thing he or she reads as instant guidance.

In the fourth place, start to get to grips with the Bible's plot line. It tells a story. Individual books fit into the story. If you have never got into the Old Testament then you don't know two thirds of the story, and are likely to misunderstand the bits you think you know. Postmodernism delights to deny overarching stories. But the whole Bible tells the unfolding plan of God's dealings with his people and his world. Why not get someone who knows the Bible well to introduce you to an overview of the whole thing? Alternatively get a book like *According To Plan* (by Graham Goldsworthy) that will help you work through the whole plot line. You will be amazed and enthralled by the scope of God's plan to rescue people.

Next, learn to ask good questions of the Bible, such as: What is actually going on in the passage? What did it mean to its original hearers? What does it mean today? (It cannot mean today what it did not mean to them!) What is God teaching me about God here? Is God teaching me anything about me here? What should I do as a result of this passage? How am I going to make sure I do it?

Then find ways to be accountable for your reading. Bible reading plans can be excellent. Sometimes they may make you feel guilty when you know you are umpteen days behind, but that doesn't mean they aren't useful tools. Talk and pray with others about what you are learning. You are more likely to do it if other people are interested in your Christian growth.

Go on to write down what you have learned. Make a note of things you don't understand in a passage and look them up.

Finally, pray through your Bible reading. Pray as you begin and ask God to help you understand his Word. Pray through what you learn and ask him to help you live out the consequences of the passages you read.

Some final questions and suggestions

To review the chapter, here are some questions and suggestions to consider:

1. What sort of effect is Postmodern thinking most likely to have on your own Bible reading?

2. In what ways does the surrounding culture most easily influence you?
3. List some of the positive things you have learned about getting into the Bible from hearing other people teach it.
4. Note one practical thing you could do this week that will help you delight in God's Word and not leave it closed any more.

Chapter 8

Postmodern Christian Living 2: The Postmodern Church?

> For the time will come when people will not put up with sound doctrine. Instead, to suit their own desires, they will gather around them a great number of teachers to say what their itching ears want to hear. They will turn their ears away from the truth and turn aside to myths.
>
> 2 Timothy 4:3–4

Have you ever been astonished at the number of magazine titles on offer at any large newsagent? It is quite possible to find a dozen magazines on mountain biking, a hundred playing on fears about health and literally thousands on lifestyle, amid a vast range on every other conceivable subject.

Since the Second World War – that is, over the same period that Modernism has been transmuting into Postmodernism – there has been a vast explosion of special interest groups, clubs and societies, reflected by the magazine culture. The scale of the explosion has a lot to do with a lack of commitment to truth. In the absence of things that we *believe* or hold to be true, we settle instead for belonging to groups with similar interests. It makes us feel good to be surrounded by groups of like-minded people.

The development of the magazine culture is a symptom of increasing tribalism and social fragmentation. Each mountain-bike magazine, for example, offers a slightly different spin and satisfies a tiny niche market. That they sell at all demonstrates that people perceive themselves and their interests according to those tiny niches. Perhaps the defining mark of our society is not something that unifies it, but its huge and accelerating fragmentation.

There is little left that constitutes core values in Western culture. The alternative is the tribe or the niche. The tribe tends to be defined by leisure activities. We understand ourselves largely in terms of our leisure. We work in order to enjoy leisure rather than for the value and enjoyment of work. For most people the best part of the week is the weekend. That is what we live for. Work exists to provide money for leisure.

The vital question for Christians to consider is to what extent we understand our local church, or indeed our Christian commitment as a whole, as a special interest group or niche leisure activity. Our modern idea of leisure didn't really exist until the 1950s because few people had surplus income. In the last half-century there has been a deliberate divide between what we see as work or the public sphere of life, and what we see as leisure or the private and individualized side of life. It seems to me that in most people's minds Christianity is kept for the weekend and is therefore a leisure activity – a highly privatized niche of specialized interest rather than universal significance – religion as a lifestyle choice.

The trouble with special interest groups is that they require no commitment. What they offer is interest and entertainment, not truth. There is nothing in the magazine culture that must be believed simply because it is true. If a group member finds they are no longer in tune with the direction of the group, there is nothing within the group to encourage commitment. There are plenty of other options on offer and every reason to leave and find something more entertaining.

The dangers of this mind-set to the life of the church are obvious and alarming. If we allow ourselves to see church as a leisure activity to pursue or a special interest group to attend, rather than as the people of God and the bride of Christ, then it is all too easy for church to become entertainment. Worship becomes spectacle; sermon becomes sound-bite. When people feel uncomfortable with a note of challenge, there is no reason not to leave and look for something more palatable. We must increasingly expect that people coming to church or exploring Christianity for the first time will come with this mind-set.

Genuine fellowship?

> The body is a unit, though it is made up of many parts; and though all its parts are many, they form one body. So it is with Christ. For we were all baptised by one Spirit into one body – whether Jews or Greeks, slave or free – and we were all given the one Spirit to drink.
>
> Now the body is not made up of one part but of many. If the foot should say, 'Because I am not a hand, I do not belong to the body,' it would not for that reason cease to be part of the body. And if the ear should say, 'Because I am not an eye, I do not belong to the body,' it would not for that reason cease to be part of the

body. If the whole body were an eye, where would the sense of hearing be? If the whole body were an ear, where would the sense of smell be? But in fact God has arranged the parts in the body, every one of them, just as he wanted them to be. If they were all one part, where would the body be? As it is, there are many parts, but one body.

The eye cannot say to the hand, 'I don't need you!' And the head cannot say to the feet, 'I don't need you!' On the contrary, those parts of the body that seem to be weaker are indispensable, and the parts that we think are less honourable we treat with special honour. And the parts that are unpresentable are treated with special modesty, while our presentable parts need no special treatment. But God has combined the members of the body and has given greater honour to the parts that lacked it, so that there should be no division in the body, but that its parts should have equal concern for each other. If one part suffers, every part suffers with it; if one part is honoured, every part rejoices with it. Now you are the body of Christ, and each one of you is a part of it.

1 Corinthians 12:12–27

The New Testament uses all sorts of images to describe the church – the household of God, a spiritual temple built on Christ, the bride of Christ, and so on. There is no space here to unpack the doctrine of the church, but it is pertinent to reflect briefly on this key passage in 1 Corinthians where Paul describes the church using language from the human body.

Paul makes two main points, each of which he then elaborates. The first is that we are baptized into the body of Christ – that is, his church – when we become believers. At that point the Holy Spirit includes us in Christ and in his body. Belonging to Christ's church is not optional; it is a given. His second point is that belonging to the body is not something we can elect to opt out of. We can no more extract ourselves from the body of Christ than a human eye can say that it doesn't want to belong to its body. Neither can we reject other believers, because this would be like an eye saying to the hand, 'I don't need you!'

The church, then, is the *community* of *believers*. A local church is the expression of the universal community of believers in a particular area. Clearly, if either element, community or belief, is missing, then you don't have a church. If a collection of people believes the gospel but denies that they or other believers have a part to play in the body of Christ, then there is no church. If there is an outward expression of community but no belief in the gospel then, similarly, there is no church, but rather a social club. In either case Christ is denied. For God has set him 'over everything for the church, which is his body' (Ephesians 1:22–23).

Genuine fellowship means that Christians are united in the gospel. The church is the community of the gospel. Even the word 'fellowship' in New Testament times had the connotation of a business partnership: a mutual commitment to shared aims, in this case the aims of believing the gospel and living the gospel in the world. 'Fellowship' definitely does not mean mere organizational unity, as various ecumenical and multi-faith movements suggest, where core beliefs are often down-played for the sake of working or worshipping together with those who hold different beliefs.

Paul's statement that we belong to the body when we are baptized by the Spirit into Christ shows us that it is the gospel, and only the gospel, that defines the church. We join the church when God enables us to hear and respond to the gospel. Genuine fellowship is therefore what happens when we believe the gospel together and act on it to serve God's purposes. A visible local church may have any number of activities, but those activities are not what defines the church. Only the gospel does that.

Of course, in a selfish, Postmodern society the two elements of church life we will be most strongly encouraged to neglect are belief and belonging. We will be pressured to down-play what it means to belong to the body and to live out God's priorities in the body. But to avoid genuine fellowship is to sacrifice our commitment to the truth of the gospel and its outworking in and through the church.

Busyness

I believe that pressure is applied in a number of ways today. First the sheer busyness of life in the modern world pushes regular church attendance down our list of priorities. Where a few years ago we might have gone to church twice on a Sunday, now it is once – or once a fortnight. It is not that belonging to Christ consists in attending meetings. Rather that when we distance ourselves from where the other Christians are, then there is little opportunity for fellowship, little concern for being built up and equipped for the service of the gospel, little edification or encouragement in evangelism.

Many professing Christians are subtly bowing to the values of the world. Faced with a choice between continuing church attendance or taking a promotion that will move us away from our church, many automatically seem to prefer the latter. When this happens it shows we haven't understood what it means to belong to the body. We find it natural to put our ambitions and ourselves ahead of the concerns of Christ.

Consumerism

We have already seen that we live at a time when the consumer is king. It is easy to treat church as a consumer product. We taste, we dabble and we 'go along' while we enjoy it. The main criterion for attending church is whether I feel that it 'meets my needs' rather than fulfilling the purposes of God. A whole raft of church-marketing strategies is one of the results. I don't want to disparage genuine attempts to make churches welcoming in order for people to hear and respond to the gospel, but the marketing of church as product can quickly become the marketing of the gospel as product. This in turn easily becomes *not* the gospel, for the simple reason that the gospel is not a consumer product. It is good news that *must* be believed and responded to because nothing else saves people. The thing most lacking in the consumer mentality is the element of challenge or discomfort. When the marketing of church takes the sting from the gospel, then it is not the gospel that we are believing or teaching. Of course, when we merely dabble with the church and with the gospel we are not really belonging at all. It is a daring pastor who preaches whole-hearted commitment in a selfish age, but as David Wells eloquently puts it: '[the church] is made, owned, impelled, authorised, guided and nourished by God in Christ. If the church loses this sense of ownership and intimate relationship – its sense of identity as God's people – then it ceases to be church.'[3]

Is it possible that there are lots of organizations which call themselves churches but are not? In the Old Testament God was not beyond withdrawing his presence and his glory from his people in Jerusalem when they ceaselessly declared by their lack of belief that they were his people no longer. When local fellowships fail to believe or live the gospel, might we not expect the glory to depart today?

In short, it is vital for the church to know what it is and what it is for. We belong to God and exist for his purposes. Christ builds the church on the Word of God through the

Spirit. We are to lovingly express this in all the content of our programmes and our preaching. We are not to be distracted. This inevitably means confronting our culture of independence and self. Rather than submitting to the values of the age – short-termism, entertainment and personal fulfilment – we must be clear and up-front about the cost of following Jesus. Commitment to the truth, lived out in the way we belong to the body of Christ, shows up a fragmenting society for what it is. We need to make clear what it means for Christ to be Lord of the church and of our lives. Preaching and living total commitment to Christ may be immensely hard today but it is immeasurably important. Anything less fails to encourage people to count the cost of discipleship and sells them a watered-down gospel. Anything else is turning from the gospel to myths which our itching ears want to hear.

Values

The key question is: do we take our values from the world or from the Word? If the former, we are not living correctly as the body of Christ. When this happens we put our own interests before those of the church or of the Lord. If I disagree with my church leaders I will naturally look for a church where I am more comfortable. If the church needs funds for a mission project but I want a new hi-fi, then I am likely to go for the hi-fi. If my church is committed to biblical teaching and a church down the road intrigues me because its style is more to my liking, then I am likely to move, even if the teaching is poor. All these things are likely if we fail to understand what it means to belong to the body. As the apostle Paul put it in the words that began this chapter, we are likely to associate with people who teach what our itching ears want to hear. And the world concurs and encourages this.

Church hopping

I meet many students in London for whom the transport networks in the city make it very easy to church hop. When asked which church they attend, many reply that they go to one church in the morning 'for the teaching' and another in the evening 'for the worship'. Not only does this betray a critical misunderstanding of worship; it shows a complete misunderstanding of church as well. It is not only churches with poor Bible teaching that fail to help people belong to the body. The same can easily be true of the big preaching-centre church where size allows anonymity. Following their graduation, it is tragic to watch some students perpetually moving around, seeking something that replaces their student church/Christian Union combination, when that combination no longer exists. These graduates find it hard to belong to a church because they have never understood or experienced what it really means to belong to the body while they are at college. They have merely been consumers and are immeasurably the poorer for not experiencing God's purpose in belonging to his family. The church too is poorer for not having them.

Worship, entertainment or therapy?

We noted in the last chapter that the level of Bible knowledge across the Christian world is dropping and dropping. We are losing our confidence that this is the pre-eminent way that God speaks. One consequence of this is that we are ceasing to define what the church is biblically, and starting to define it in terms of our feelings and experience.

Now I certainly do not want to say that feelings are unimportant in our Christian lives and devotion to God. Quite the opposite. The risen Christ wrote a letter to the church in Ephesus in Revelation 2 commending them for being doctrinally correct and hard-working but chastising them for having lost their first love. It is a devastating critique of a church that looks thoroughly biblical on the outside but has lost its heart for the Lord. They are no longer passionate about Jesus. They are taken up with correctness rather than overflowing with love for him. In all I am about to say I am not advocating that we become dry and doctrinaire.

The fact remains, however, that though feelings and affections are vital in our Christian lives, they are an incredibly poor way to define the value of our experience of church, or how acceptable to God a particular style of praise is. By definition our feelings change. We can be up one day and down the next. If we measure our church life by how well our feelings are served, we will find ourselves on a real roller-coaster.

Moreover, we will also tend to pursue short-term fixes and things that excite our feelings and heighten our emotions rather than feed our minds. Whether or not we believe that there is a contemporary gift of prophecy, it is easy to go a step too far and say that we expect something other than the voice of the Spirit, through the Bible, to be the main or normal way we experience the work of God in our church life. The danger is that, combined with a lack of confidence in Scripture, we simply desire the excitement of supposedly instant access to some vaguely defined spiritual experience. We then reject anything that looks like it requires hard work or commitment – such as serious preaching or Bible study. Again, this is symptomatic of our putting more trust in feelings than in truth, and more confidence in a subjective 'now' word than in God's revealed eternal Word.

All of which brings us to the subject of worship, in relation to Postmodern culture. It is clear from the Bible that worship is a very broad term that includes the whole of our lives lived out before God and under the authority of God's Word. Worship includes singing but is much bigger than that. It is closely related to our desire to bring our lives and actions in line with God's truth. In other words, God is the object of worship and he is worshipped acceptably and truly when we are living in line with his revealed will and proclaiming his truth with our lives as well as with our lips. Worship thus has a highly objective component – we affirm that God is who he is in our worship. We admit that he has authority and proclaim the wonder of his deeds. We respond to the holiness of his character and bow before the splendour of his glory. And then we place ourselves under him in obedient love and awe. Worship is massively about God, and not about me.

When put down on paper like this, few Christians would disagree about the heart of worship. Yet in our practice do we not frequently reduce worship to singing? Now singing is not bad – indeed it is very good. While there are few New Testament examples of sung worship, particularly congregational sung worship, there certainly are examples of people singing praise to God. But we live in an age where truth is denied and feelings are held up as of immense value. In an age like this we must recognize the fact that singing is inherently an emotional activity. It rightly engages our feelings. But we must therefore ask hard questions about what we are singing in order to ensure that it is in line with objective and biblical concepts of worship. Unless we worship and respond to God as he really is, then our worship is unacceptable or even idolatrous.

So what about the songs we sing? I never cease to be amazed at some of the lyrics, both old and new, that we sing unthinkingly. If many were written down and presented to us as doctrinal statements we would quickly throw them away, but when they come as songs with catchy tunes they get in under our defences. Someone has quipped that we are much more likely to sing heresy than to speak it.

In these circumstances should we not carefully examine the trend of many modern songs to be privatized, emotional, subjective and individualized responses to the Lord? We must not discourage personal response, but we must encourage right response that engages with who God really is. Once again David Wells is helpful on this subject. On a comparison between several books of hymns and songs from a generation ago with several from today he notes that God's moral character, our sin and the corporate nature of the church are down-played today compared with then.[4] The reason, he suggests, is that much recent material gives no doctrinal justification for the praise it offers. As a result, it is very easy to replace God's concerns for the proclamation of his person, his truth and the response of penitence and holiness that he desires, with romantic imagery and our own desire for psychological wholeness.

Now this is quite a scathing critique. There is much modern material that I like and use regularly. But Dr Wells does show how necessary it is for all of us to carefully examine the songs we sing, asking the question, 'Is this worshipping God as the Bible actually reveals him?' Unless we do, our choices of songs will be dictated more by feeling than by biblical reality.

How do we measure up here? An interesting question to ask about songs is, 'Is this song more about God than about me?' A disturbing proportion of recent material is clearly more about me than it is about God. 'I' am often the subject of most verbs – how I exult in God, what I am going to do for him, how I feel about him. It is not that such songs don't have their place but that it is not the primary place. If they come top of the list, above proclaiming and adoring God, then they are not worship but egotism.

Our conclusion must be to pick songs primarily not on musical or feeling grounds but on theological ones. If we fail to do this, then worship easily becomes Postmodern personal therapy, all about the pursuit of wholeness and not about thankfulness for who God is, for forgiveness of sins or hope of heaven. Jesus told us that the Father desires those who worship in spirit and in truth (John 4) and that worshippers like these are true worshippers. The flip side of the coin is that it is possible to offer unacceptable or false worship because it is not worship in spirit and in truth.

A final note on worship in a Postmodern context concerns the contemporary phenomenon of the 'worship leader'. Just as there is little New Testament concept of congregational sung worship, so there is no New Testament office or understanding of the worship leader. Worship, at least in Acts, was much more closely allied to bearing witness in the Temple to the apostles' teaching and sharing in the life of the body together, house to house. If there was a New Testament act of leading worship, then those engaged in it were the apostles and it centred not around song but around the ministry of the Word and prayer. The twelve apostles are not around today and their ministry was a unique and unrepeatable ministry. But if we grant that it is helpful for someone to take the responsibility of leading worship in the congregation, we should always make the following conditions in the light of being distinctive in a Postmodern culture.

The first is that such a responsibility is primarily a ministry of the Word and prayer, especially in the choice of songs and other material. It is inappropriate for a prayerless person to lead. It is also inappropriate to give this responsibility to someone who has no desire to work at leading worship biblically.

The second condition is that people are not necessarily qualified for the job simply on the basis of being good musicians. Nor is leading a congregation in praise, at root, a musical activity. Indeed, acceptable praise to God does not *need* to contain music at all.

The third condition is that it is wrong for worship leaders to have the major stake in establishing the ethos of an entire fellowship, unless they are also the church leader. Worship styles and preferences must be secondary to the ministry of the Word. Far too few people see that the way we listen and respond to a biblical sermon is as much an act of worship as singing. Maybe even more so.

A fourth condition is that anyone given the responsibility of leading worship must be firmly under the authority of church leaders, and under the ministry of the Word. It is great to have gifted musicians and music leaders in any church, but there is no specifically stated New Testament ministry of worship leading. I have been in a few situations where people given this job have seen it as a God-given and inalienable right for them and them alone to lead because they, in some sense, have a special anointing to do so. This is very close to a personality cult. It is interesting to see among many young people that those held in high regard today are worship leaders and musicians rather than preachers.

This chapter is a plea to ensure that we are biblical and truth-orientated in all our church life together. Everything we do must flow from what God has revealed. It seems likely that the current trend to individualism and subjectivity in the worship life of the church has arisen out of a helpful emphasis on rediscovering every-member ministry. In many fellowships it is now normal for everyone to be encouraged to participate and bring individual contributions to enrich the body. This must be right. But it makes it very important for leaders and ministers to help everyone to bring contributions that are biblical and of eternal relevance rather than merely trite.

It is no good to assume that we are honouring God if we cannot tell whether or not the content of our worship is biblical. The health of the church now and in the future depends on being godly in everything we do. If a congregation fails to stand for truth now, we can have no confidence that the Lord will not withdraw. And if we don't stand for truth, who will?

Some final questions

1. List the people who take an active interest in your Christian growth. If you cannot think of any, list some people whom you might possibly approach to encourage you. This is seeking genuine fellowship.
2. Write down your five favourite hymns or worship songs. Then write down the reasons why you like each of them. Are the reasons subjective (i.e. to do with your feelings or the ability to express how you feel to God) or objective (i.e. reflecting on God's eternal character and truth)? Both are important, but to have only the first to the exclusion of the second is alarmingly Postmodern.
3. Can you vocalize your church's vision and the part you play in fulfilling it? If not, is this because (a) it doesn't have one that anyone is aware of, or (b) you are not aware what part you should play, or (c) for whatever reason, you are deliberately not involved?

Chapter 9
The Immorality of Postmodernism

The power of pragmatism

Recently I chatted to a friend who teaches English at a British university. My friend, a professor, is responsible for teaching, writing and popularizing some of the most radical Postmodern thinking in the market-place of ideas today. Having not seen him for a while, I asked how he was. His answer took me by surprise. He admitted to being increasingly frustrated by the huge number of students coming to study Postmodern theory at post-graduate level who, in his words, are now entirely pragmatic in their world-view. He was concerned that few show finely honed critical faculties and few are able to engage with the subject-matter at any real depth. 'I can tell that in a few years, when I retire,' he said, 'I will not want to teach this any more.'

It was a staggering admission. For his concern that students come to study for purely pragmatic reasons – not for learning itself but merely for the prospects it opens up – is a Postmodern self-fulfilling prophecy. Several years ago I spent a year studying under my friend, during which he tried to convince me that, in a relativistic world, no one system of value is any more true or valuable than any other system of value, that claims about truth are only valuable to the person or culture that makes them. In his view there is no such thing as universal truth. Therefore what matters is simply what works for getting on with others or for making life seem good.

This is more or less bound to produce pragmatic students. It is exactly what Postmodernists have been predicting will happen for years. It is the logical conclusion of an ideology that is suspicious of value judgments. Now that my friend is facing the consequences of the theory, it suddenly seems less attractive.

I put this to him. He asked, 'Are you blaming me for the pragmatism?' I was. For what is taught in universities today is common currency amongst everyone tomorrow, as students and media professionals take the values they have imbibed and spread them far and wide.

What we are seeing is a prevailing world-view that is completely pragmatic. If it feels good, do it. If it doesn't seem to hurt anyone, it's okay. If it is not actually illegal, then I can do what I want. And if it is illegal but I still want to do it, then my desires probably take priority. This is pragmatism. It is everywhere. It is just what we should expect, of course, when society looks on truthful authority as an unethical power game or as intrusive control over our lives.

Of course, to deny authority and enshrine self was at the heart of Modernism before it was at the heart of Postmodernism. Modernism denies that God exists or that he provides external standards to which we must conform. It does so through appealing to science to try to explain the world without God. Postmodernism denies that God exists by casting doubt on meaning and truth: two different strategies but with the same goal – to envisage a world without God, in which we can deny the need to live under God's authority. Granted, to the Postmodern theorist it is rather more complicated than this, and many also want to deny that individuals have any significance or authority. The rejection of the significance of people, however, flows from the denial of authority, which in turn flows directly from the denial of God. Nietzsche was the first to proclaim that God is dead, and we are all living with the consequences. All that is left, it seems, is pragmatism.

Pragmatism and morality

My contention is that what my friend sees at an academic level, and what we see all around us, is first and foremost a moral phenomenon. Postmodernism is a moral condition – or rather an immoral one. Postmodern rejection of authority is a rejection of morality. It says that it is all right for people to think quite differently about an issue like human sexuality or abortion. All sides of the discussion are equally legitimate and we should never say that some are right or that others are wrong. To do that is to impose authority. Far from existing in the rarefied realm of universities, Postmodernism affects us all at the level of daily decision-making about right and wrong. Whenever we ask somebody's opinion about a decision, or some matter of wider concern in the news, and receive the well-worn apathetic reply, 'Whatever', we see the result of Postmodernism. Not only has it created a society where people really don't care about things that ought to matter, but also one in which they have no framework to decide on matters of right and wrong, other than the intensely personal and subjective criterion, 'Do I feel good about this?' It really is true that people have stopped having significant conversations about things that genuinely matter and have replaced deep communication with trivia.

Rejection of authority is the rejection of right and wrong – not simply disagreement on what is right or wrong in a particular situation, but rejection of the idea that right and wrong exist as correct ways to think or act. How could it be otherwise in a relativistic world? Christians believe, however, that we live in a deeply moral universe, a universe whose very existence depends on the creative acts of God. He defines what is good and what is evil by his very character. Christians cannot, by definition, be either relativist or apathetic on matters of right and wrong. For that is an affront to the character of God. It is this affront that stands at the heart of Postmodernism's opposition to Christianity.

Isn't Postmodernism just playful?

Following a recent article on the importance of believing in and proclaiming truth, I received a letter from an aggrieved correspondent. The writer believes she is a Christian and may be. She roundly questioned whether I understood anything at all about Postmodernism or had read anything about contemporary theory or culture. She believed that nothing she had read suggests that Postmodernism is anything more than a creative and playful way of thinking that encourages her to see the world as fodder for amusement.

She has imbibed many of the surface manifestations of Postmodernism – its anti-foundational nature, its desire to subvert existing norms and scorn existing authority structures, its ironic and amusing tone – but without asking the deeper question about why Postmodernism has those things on the surface.

After all, on the face of it there is little wrong with much literature that plays with existing norms, little wrong with tackling some political issues with a bit of a satirical wink, and little wrong with the act of questioning received ideas about what we believe. As Christians we would want to affirm the value of at least some of those things. But she never asked the 'Why?' question.

Asking the 'Why?' question

Why is Postmodernism anti-foundational? Why is irony the overwhelming way in which Postmodern writing chooses to examine the world? Why is Postmodernism questioning received beliefs? If the answer to these questions was 'In order to ascertain truth and to live by it', then Christians would answer with a hearty 'Amen.' But it is plainly and clearly obvious that this is not the reason at all. The reason why Postmoderns are anti-foundational is that they have pre-decided that there is no such thing as meaning, or at least no objective meaning. The reason why the main Postmodern mode of writing is irony is not merely to have fun, although fun it may be. The reason is that the theorists have pre-decided that as 'the author is dead', then by writing in ironic ways they hope to empower the reader to bring their own interpretations to the text, making it mean what they wish. The reader is king now.

My concern for my correspondent is that she is happy to dabble with Postmodernism, entirely unaware of the basis on which it is built. This is increasingly common. At an academic level it is rare for undergraduates to be encouraged to examine the theoretical foundations of all they are taught. They are taught it as truth, and are expected to believe it without question and regurgitate it for good marks. Underlying suppositions are rarely exposed below post-graduate level. At a popular level, people increasingly believe what they do about the world without ever questioning their foundations. Maybe it was always so. Perhaps the church has sometimes even contributed to the malaise by discouraging inquisitive and adventurous thinking. But, for many, Postmodern culture is simply the water in which we swim, a solution of weak acid subtle enough to go unnoticed but immensely corrosive given time to do its work.

Compartmentalized values

I have met and talked to many non-Christian medical students in the course of my work. Medical studies are often the last bastion of scientific Modernism in universities. After all, nobody wants to be operated on by a Postmodern surgeon! Medics know the vital need for objective knowledge when making a diagnosis and the dreadful dangers that go with speculation. Yet if you get these professional Modernists chatting in the bar about personal values, you will find that most of them are just as much at sea as anyone else. This failure to hold values that are the same privately as professionally is confused at best and terribly inconsistent and hypocritical at worst.

Without doubt this sort of split in values models Postmodernism to a tee. It simply isn't necessary to be consistent any more. It might even be seen as more virtuous to be inconsistent, to hold values and beliefs privately that never encroach on public or professional life.

A last word about my letter writer. While she, and others, continue to see Postmodernism as a tool of playful creativity and nothing more, they stand in great danger. Because, as we will see further, Postmodernism is morally corrosive in its denial of the authority of God and the uniqueness of Jesus. If we fail to see this, it is hard to see how we might avoid the subtle slide into being playful with moral values, the enticement to increasingly question the authority of the Bible or the powerful pull of self-gratification. That is the whole thing about Postmodern ideas of 'play'. Play, in this sense, is about self-gratification, about trivializing content and meaning, about confusing issues of truth and communication, about taking the world lightly, about enjoyment in the game and little more.

The need for discernible content

I was fascinated by the response to a seminar I ran at a British arts festival which claims to have a Christian basis. I was speaking on a Christian approach to Foucault and Derrida. Two people enthusiastically chatted afterwards. They were postgraduate students who were delighted to find someone thinking about these writers. Both were extremely positive about Derrida and his ideas of the play of significance and meaning. Both were negative about the idea that things can mean something in a way that can be communicated. Neither was keen to talk about the Bible or about whether God reveals both information and himself in knowable ways. Both, however, claimed to be Christians, but with almost no discernible Christian content to their belief about God or about the Bible. For them 'Christian' was a pragmatic label that they attached to a desirable lifestyle or admirable behaviour. They didn't think you actually have to believe anything.

Interestingly, after the seminar another man came to take extreme issue with my claim that Scripture is authoritative. He told me he had once been a pastor but had become disillusioned both with the ministry and with the Bible when he had read about God's wrath in the Old Testament. He believed that it was unacceptable for anyone to hold that these things are true in today's culture.

These two responses go together. In the second case the man was not free from authority; he had merely chosen to replace the authority of Scripture with the demands of contemporary culture. He did so entirely for reasons of personal comfort. He did not wish to have a God who judges. It followed that if the Bible says that God judges, then he must get rid of the Bible. Yet he called himself a

Christian. And the two students started by disbelieving the Bible and built up their structure for living and thinking from there, labelling it 'Christian'.

Whose authority are we under?

If we get rid of the Bible, and if we refuse to deal with the God who is there as he really is, then what we have got is *not* Christian. The way we then live is *not* Christian. It might be an attempt to live a good life, but that is not what being a Christian means. The authority under which we then live is *not* Christian, but rather the values of the world.

A few weeks ago I tuned in to a programme on prime-time British TV called *The God List.* It made for disturbing viewing. The idea was to get a panel of judges to put forward a list of 'the fifty most influential people of faith in Britain'. As you can imagine, they came up with a mixed bunch! From Cliff Richard to the Dalai Lama, from Tony Blair to Nicky Gumbel, from Prince Charles to the Archbishop of Canterbury. Two things were notable about the programme. Firstly, the criteria by which anyone made it on to the list were predictably vague, and secondly, it was repeated time and time again that faith is 'not about the content of belief, but about the way we behave in this society'. Or in other words, it doesn't matter what you believe, only what you do. Of course, this is the only way to make a programme like this today.

The God List depends on there being no qualitative difference between each person's beliefs. They are all seen as equally valid because all seem to help people behave correctly and be good citizens. Only one person, the Christian businessman Ken Costa, was bold enough to say that his faith was not a private matter. 'My work-station is my place of worship,' he argued. Mr Costa is one of the leading lights behind the Alpha Course. Alpha was given a passably good write-up by the programme makers, though it was labelled as the most significant new marketing opportunity for the Church of England in recent years. Even evangelism, the programme told us, is nothing more than a marketing exercise, a new brand name for the Christian product on the supermarket shelf.

Defining faith

Of course, the programme's conclusions, which might be summarized as 'Faith [in an undefined sort of way] makes you good', are completely at sea. The Bible is abundantly clear that faith in God, trusting his promises, believing his revelation of himself and acting in accordance with it, is good because it is true. It is the true response that God desires of us. But the Bible is equally clear that putting faith in anything else is not a helpful means to spiritual values for life, but rebellion and an affront to God. That is why we must never take the line that the multitude of world religions shows that everybody is seeking after God. To the contrary, the existence of a multitude of religions shows that many are running away from God and making idols for themselves that God despises.

This second sort of faith is not good. It is bad because it is untrue, because it has false content or no content to its beliefs and because it neither leads people to acknowledge God humbly, nor to find salvation in Christ. This sort of faith is not saving faith but fatal faith. But it is popular. Which is why Christians must be clear on the content of what we believe and clear on the good reasons for believing it.

Lord Melvyn Bragg, the well-known British television presenter and journalist, presented a series on 2000 years of Christianity to mark the Millennium. I saw only a few episodes in which he sympathetically chaired discussion about a variety of subjects related to Christianity. Each episode introduced a number of guests, some Christian, others not. The programme that sticks in my mind involved Gore Vidal in discussion with a Roman Catholic Archbishop. Lord Bragg repeatedly invited the bishop to give some explanation of why Christianity was true and why we should be Christians. This the bishop declined to do or was unable to do. The best he could manage was to say that he was unable to explain the content of Christianity to the audience or persuade them that it was true unless they discovered it by joining 'the community of faith'. Or, in other words, that there is no content that is demonstrable to the world. We must just believe it, apparently, despite the bishop's total lack of evidence, exposure or explanation, discovering later whether it is true or not after having joined the Roman Catholic Church. Needless to say, Gore Vidal ran rings around the bishop, and rightly so. The bishop had no answer to give for why he has the faith that he does. This response is entirely inadequate. As we have said, it is no good just being clear on the content of the Christian message (and the bishop wasn't); it is vital that we are able to explain *why* we believe the content to be reliable and true. Without this we fall into a mysticism that is nothing more than a spiritual spin on relativism.

Let me summarize where we have got to so far. Postmodernism is a moral phenomenon. It denies authority and meaning. It refutes any idea of revelation. These two things sum up the affront of Postmodernism to Christianity. Christians believe that life is meaningful because God made it so and has revealed it so. Christians believe that people are meaningful because we are created in God's image and for relationship with him. Christians believe that it is God as Creator who defines, in himself and by his character, what is right and wrong. The act of denying authority, meaning and revelation removes any reference to God, and by definition any reference to the standard of what constitutes good and bad. We are back to William Golding again: 'If God is dead, if man is the highest, then good and evil are decided by majority vote.' How could it be otherwise?

Postmodernism brings moral destitution in its wake. It is immoral for at least three reasons. The first is that, in refusing God and denying truth, it denies objective standards of right and wrong. Secondly, in making the self the only possible arbiter of good or bad behaviour, it affirms that individuals are free to do things that, in any objective light, are dreadful and says that this is good for them. Thirdly, enthroning the individual means that nobody has the right to offer a challenge to evil. This is the effect of the new tolerance. We used to be able to disagree with someone while simultaneously affirming their rights to think differently; this was true tolerance. Postmodern tolerance, on the other hand, tells us that to challenge the views of another is to affront their personhood and deny their fundamental human rights.

Yet if the individual is the highest, then individual satisfaction defines what is right – and denies anyone the right to say anything to the contrary. This is little short of tyranny. The irony is that Postmodernists accuse Christians of playing power games. But here is, in effect, a relativist metanarrative that is more conforming, more oppressive, and more morally indifferent than any power play yet conceived. Postmodernists now deem the very word 'morality' to be useless because they recognize that morality depends on a moral law-giver to define right and wrong. Instead they use the word 'ethics', which they take to mean simply how we live with others in a society without moral givens.

All of this leaves societies in moral collapse, no longer believing that anything has universal value or significance. It leaves people who are hostile to any Christian claim that God has authority and must be obeyed.

The effect of moral collapse on individuals

Pause now to consider the following far-reaching questions:

1. What sort of effects should we expect to see on people in a world that increasingly cannot distinguish between right and wrong?
2. How do people handle guilt in a Postmodern setting?
3. Does relativism offer any hope for stable human relationships? Why, or why not?
4. A student friend tells you that a lecturer has offered to give a higher mark for an essay if she removes the parts that express strong personal values and writes something more liberal. How would you tell her to respond? How would you encourage her to justify this response?

Hostility to God

It should come as no surprise that people are apathetic and hostile to the things of God, because nobody believes anything any more. Or rather, it has become fashionable to believe any nonsense that comes along if it makes us feel good. Feelings are the only thing to go on when the goalposts of good and evil are removed.

Of course, this has applications for the whole of life. In a discussion with a collection of Postmodern theorists on the work of Michel Foucault, I asked what they made of his crusadingly gay lifestyle. The answer boiled down to 'Whatever was good for him.' Later in that same discussion I ventured the idea that, although Foucault's situation was complex, his beliefs and behaviour went some way to creating the moral and medical conditions that killed him. He died of AIDS. I have never met in any situation such a vehement response! I was told that I was anti-gay, anti-people with AIDS, and how could I possibly say that anyone who had died of AIDS after championing individual freedom, as Foucault did, did anything wrong!

I certainly don't want to suggest that Postmodern belief leads directly to child abuse. There are plenty of other reasons for moral failure and sin is a much larger phenomenon than Postmodernism! But it is still the case that Postmodern theory has no way of judging such behaviour to be wrong. The fact remains that Foucault pursued his relativism to the ultimate degree and the moral consequences killed him. He behaved this way because he believed this way. Postmodern rejection of God affects our behaviour.

Morality and individual preference

Foucault defines right and wrong entirely according to individual preference. This is the second effect of moral collapse that we should expect to see on individuals. There is nobody we trust to say what is right and wrong. Moral criteria have been replaced by wants and desires. The trouble is, as in the case of Foucault, that our wants and desires are frequently selfish and unholy. Naturally we do not seek God. Naturally we go the other way.

From the very first entry of sin into the world we have tried to deny our guilt. When Adam and Eve ate the fruit in the garden God confronted them with their rebellion and gave them the opportunity to confess it to him. Instinctively they went in the opposite direction. Adam blamed Eve and God – 'the woman you put here with me …' 'It isn't my fault, God. She tempted me, and you are the one who put her here. It's her fault, it's your fault. But it isn't my fault.' Eve did the same.

At the heart of relativism is the denial of sin. No behaviour is wrong; it is simply culturally conditioned. We cannot challenge any action or artefact because they are right in the culture that produced them. To challenge someone's culture is the only taboo left for the Postmodernist. Other cultures are seen as alien, with a different language, different sets of norms, different sets of rights and wrongs, completely outside our ability to comment on them or critique them. To do so is arrogance.

Denying sin

This, however, is simply to disguise and deny sinfulness. Sin means transgressing God's moral boundaries. Sin makes us morally offensive to God and guilty before him. If, however, we replace God with self, then we redefine sin not as moral transgression that offends God but as anything that offends me. We do not have to look hard for examples of how our society trivializes sin. We redefine abortion as the right to choose. It is no longer a sin, therefore, to kill a foetus but it is a sin to deny an individual's right to choose to do so. 'Sin' is reduced to the level of excess calories in a weight-loss plan. We simply don't use the vocabulary of sin any more because nobody thinks we sin. 'Other people might sin, the bad people, murderers and rapists and those who take part in ethnic cleansing. But surely *I* don't sin?' We prioritize personal fulfilment over right and wrong. At the heart of this is the suppression of sin and the need to disguise moral guilt. We only get away with it by denying what we are really like and turning away from the only one who can put us right.

It is fascinating to watch how the therapy industry has experienced explosive growth in our time. David Wells helpfully makes the point that shame is the way I feel about myself in this society.[5] Shame has replaced guilt, which depends on an understanding of objective wrong, especially objective wrong before a holy God. *Guilt* shows the deficiency in my relationship to him, *shame* highlights only my relationship with myself. The answer to guilt is the cross of Jesus Christ where sin is forgiven and sinners are reconciled to God. The answer to shame is self-actualization and therapy. We tell ourselves that we are not morally defective, we simply haven't grown or experienced enough as a person. We aren't in tune enough with ourselves. Surely if we rediscover, as a society, the extraordinary forgiveness and complete reconciliation with God that Jesus achieved on the cross, it would ring the death knell for the therapy industry.

To conclude, when we are told that there are no moral goal-posts, when all that is seen as exciting and avant-garde pushes the boundaries of moral acceptability and when churches are soft on the gospel of sin and judgment and rescue, a generation arises that has no idea about right and wrong. We have a church youth club that attracts many teenagers from around the area who clearly have no idea at all why they shouldn't abuse each other and themselves and no idea how to handle conflict except through retribution. This is no surprise! When those supposed to be in authority in the nation no longer believe anything, there is no reason why anyone else should know why stealing or abortion or violence is wrong. There is no ground to stand on except personal preference and gut feeling.

The effect of moral collapse on society

Clearly, the moral influence of Postmodernism on individuals is profound, but it also has knock-on effects on society.

Pause again to consider some more questions with far-reaching implications:

1. What sort of effects should we expect to see on society in a world that increasingly does not distinguish between right and wrong?
2. What do you make of our tendency to blame some-

one else for everything? How is Postmodernism related to the blame culture?

3. Does relativism offer any hope for a stable society? Why (or why not)?
4. On an issue such as euthanasia, why is the law not as effective for making good decisions as moral character?

Unenforceable Virtue

I am indebted to Dr David Wells for his excellent threefold description of society.[6] Wells suggests that at opposite ends of the spectrum of behaviour in society lie Law and Licence. At one end behaviour is controlled by the rigid imposition of Law. At the other end there is no control over behaviour at all.

These two are separated from each other by what he calls 'Unenforceable Virtue'. Social life should exist in this area of Unenforceable Virtue, between the two extremes of Law and Licence. In the area of Unenforceable Virtue we don't suffer the extremes of either a legal system that suppresses freedom or the anarchy of everyone expressing their freedom in absolutely any way they choose. In this area not everything goes but neither does Law control behaviour. Instead it is controlled by Unenforceable Virtue – the desire to be virtuous, not because virtue is imposed on us, but because virtuous is the right and moral thing to be. By definition Unenforceable Virtue cannot be imposed on us; we have to want to be virtuous. The reason we do not flaunt our freedom if we live in the area of Unenforceable Virtue is that we exercise self-restraint according to *moral* principles.

So why would we want to be virtuous or to act according to duty, conscience or social obligation? We only desire to behave in these ways if we believe in them. This central

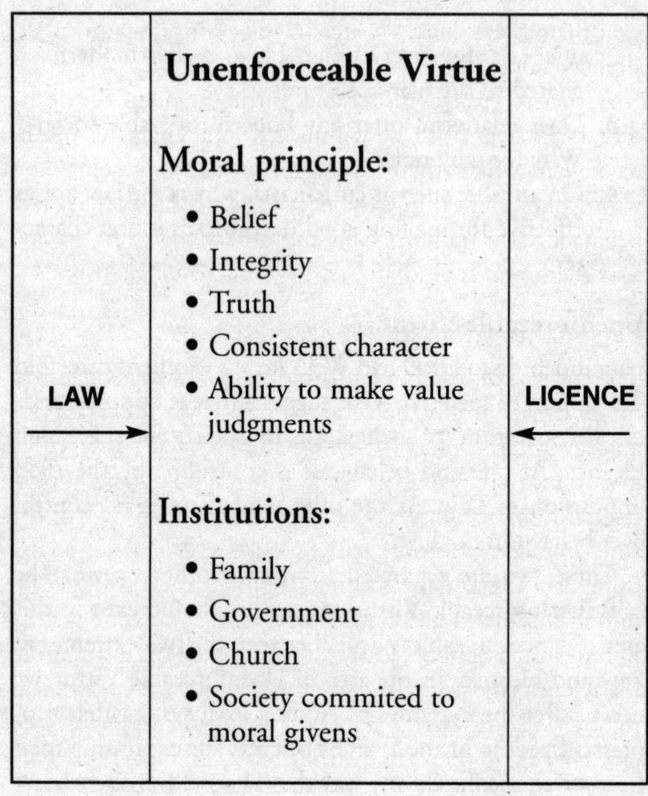

space of Unenforceable Virtue depends on moral belief. If we are to have a society that affirms truth and practices private virtue such as decency, honesty and duty, if we are to grow children and citizens of moral character and integrity, we cannot avoid the centrality of moral belief, nor the centrality of the Lord, the guarantor of right and wrong. When we leave God out of the equation things do not all go wrong instantly. However, there is an inexorable slide towards a society with no right or wrongs, with no Unenforceable Virtue. It is hard not to draw the conclusion that, as a society, we are already a long way down the slippery slope.

A society of Unenforceable Virtue is defined by the moral character of those within it. Moral character means recognizing that there are right value judgments and wrong ones, right things to believe and wrong ones, correct behaviour that honours God and others and sinful behaviour that offends God and destroys ourselves and others.

Personal freedom and moral restraint

The collapse of belief in God, and the following collapse of moral belief, means that Unenforceable Virtue is fast disappearing. Freedom of the individual is held to be more important than restraint. There is much talk about fundamental human rights, largely driven by pressure from the American Constitution which, once it enshrines something as a fundamental human right, is irreversibly committed to uphold and defend that right. No wonder that, in the United States at least, there is so much pressure from many minority groups to have their concerns recognized as rights. As soon as this happens they can never again be challenged and they can use the Law to suppress those who think differently.

If we remove Unenforceable Virtue, then, all things are allowable as long as they are not illegal. The Law is the only means to define what is not appropriate, and even the Law is only defined by society. Under this scheme, if society changes the Law, then what is right and wrong changes with it. The age-old idea that Law should be based on unchanging absolutes – in Britain, for instance, on God's revealed standards in the Ten Commandments – is undermined. Law, and hence behaviour, is only as stable as the virtue of the people who make the Law. If the Law defines morality, then what is moral will differ tomorrow from today.

The general effect is to place the individual above the Law and above society. There are untold examples of individuals setting out to change laws that they do not like – sometimes properly, at other times out of self-interest. The very fact that this is possible is seen by some as a vital freedom. We should certainly be free to change unjust laws. My concern is, exactly who defines 'unjust', and on what basis? If unjust simply means 'something I do not like' or 'something that curtails my freedom', then all we are doing in changing the Law is placing the individual above society and the idea of personal rights above that of personal responsibilities. Service of others, commitment, integrity (which depends on behaving tomorrow as I say I will today, on me not changing my mind) and self-sacrifice are greatly reduced.

Dr Wells comments that many major social institutions traditionally existed in the realm of Unenforceable Virtue – the family, the church and private moral belief, to name just three. With the collapse of moral belief, the power of these institutions as anchors and guarantors of society is reduced. That this is happening is obvious. Church attendance, at least in the UK, is reaching new lows and most people simply don't think we have anything relevant to say any more (sadly, it seems that this is true of some churches). Family breakdown is at an all-time high, bringing with it the growth in litigation, the divorce industry, pre-nuptial agreements and counselling services. In the UK the Child Support Agency, the government body tasked with ensuring that absent fathers meet child maintenance payments, was the subject of national scandal as their backlog of work grew to monumental proportions and the system broke down amid allegations of prejudice and unfair use of the Law against fathers.

Of course, if you remove Unenforceable Virtue from society, then Law is the *only* mechanism left for trying to enforce behaviour. Law has replaced those other institutions of virtue. In a recent case, twins who had been adopted over the internet were taken from their British adopted parents in the dead of night by officers of the Law, with no consultation. The natural mother in the United States had previously 'sold' the twins to two different couples. The natural father was not involved. Regardless of the rights or wrongs in this complicated and tragic case, the fact is that all parties resorted first to Law rather than to communication. The very act of doing so says something about whether the children's best interests were really the key consideration. Both adopting couples went to Law. The mother went to Law to retrieve the children, regardless of promises she had previously made and money she had received. The natural father, rather understandably, went to Law in a desperate attempt to recover his children.

In a moral society Law is the last resort, not the first response. Yet we have lost any means to deal with conflicting freedoms apart from the courts. In a society obsessed with personal freedoms and rights, the courts become the mechanism to express victimhood and to abrogate responsibility. No thinking person can be comfortable with such a litigious society. On UK television there are an increasing number of commercials for accident litigators working on a no-win, no-fee basis. 'Have you had an accident that wasn't your fault? Where there is blame there is a claim.' Whatever happened to long-suffering, humility, forgiveness and concern for justice? They are all being replaced by greed.

Conclusions

Reflecting upon the far-reaching implications of the themes we have discussed in this chapter is a huge task. In which areas do you see the effects of relativism, pluralism and individualism making a moral impact on individuals, society and the church? Why not make a list, and then pray over it.

We should all be deeply concerned to live out thoughtful Christian moral beliefs in our relationships and in our society. The only answer to moral collapse is the truth about God. The necessary response of people who turn their back on God is for them to hear and respond to the truth, repenting and bowing the knee to Christ. The way this happens is when they hear Christians preaching and speaking the good news about Jesus and see us daily living it out. It is vital that we develop a Christian mind about our culture and society, that we behave with integrity, and that we look for opportunities to engage our society with the gospel. We are, in Paul's words, ambassadors for Christ (2 Corinthians 5), and God is making his appeal through us. Let's not be poor ambassadors.

> As the scripture says, 'Anyone who trusts in him will never be put to shame' … 'Everyone who calls on the name of the Lord will be saved.' How, then, can they call on the one they have not believed in? And how can they believe in the one of whom they have not heard? And how can they hear without someone preaching to them? And how can they preach unless they are sent? As it is written, 'How beautiful are the feet of those who bring good news!'
>
> Romans 10:11–15

Chapter 10
TV and Moral Collapse

Dear Tech Support:

Last year I upgraded from Girlfriend 7.0 to Wife 1.0 and noticed that the new program began unexpected child processing that took up a lot of space and valuable resources. No mention of this phenomenon was included in the product brochure. In addition, Wife 1.0 installs itself into all other programs and launches during system initialization, where it monitors all other system activity. Applications such as Poker night 10.3, Bar Night 2.5, Weekend Golf 6.1 and Football 5.0 no longer run, crashing the system whenever selected.

In addition, applications such as Garbage Out 3.3 and Yard Work 2.1 have gone from select-as-needed to continuous schedule. Ignoring them causes Night-on-the-Couch 1.0 to take over all activity. I cannot seem to keep Wife 1.0 in the background while attempting to run some of my other favourite applications. In addition the uninstall does not work on this program. Can you help me, please!!

Thanks,

A Troubled User

Dear Troubled User:

This is a very common complaint which is mostly due to a primary misconception. Many people upgrade from Girlfriend 7.0 to Wife 1.0 with the idea that Wife 1.0 is merely a *utilities and entertainment* program. Wife 1.0 is an *operating system* and was designed by its creator to run everything. It is unlikely you would be able to purge Wife 1.0 and still convert back to Girlfriend 7.0. Hidden operating files within your system would cause Girlfriend 7.0 to emulate Wife 1.0 so nothing is gained. It is impossible to uninstall, delete, or purge the program files from the system once installed.

Some have tried to install Girlfriend 8.0 or Wife 2.0 but end up with more problems than the original system. Look in your manual under 'Warnings-Alimony/Child Support'. I recommend you keep Wife 1.0 and just deal with the situation. I suggest installing background application program C:\YES DEAR to alleviate software augmentation.

Having Wife 1.0 installed myself, I might also suggest you read the entire section regarding General Partnership Faults (GPFs). You must assume all responsibility for faults and problems that might occur, regardless of their cause. The best course of action will be to enter the command C:\APOLOGIZE. In any case avoid excessive use of YES DEAR because ultimately you will have to give the APOLOGIZE command before the operating system will return to normal. The system will run smoothly as long as you take the blame for all the GPFs.

Wife 1.0 is a great program, but very high maintenance. Consider buying additional software to improve the performance of Wife 1.0. I recommend Flowers 2.1 and Diamonds 5.0. Do not, under any circumstances, install Pretty Secretary 3.3. This is not a supported application for Wife 1.0 and is likely to cause irreversible damage to the operating system.

Best of luck,

Tech Support

Anonymous, from a forwarded email

Personal identity in a media age

I chuckled when I received the above email. There can be few people who regularly use the internet who don't receive such humorous forwards. This one caught my eye for more than its humour, however. Although it takes a jaunty look at relationships in the modern world, confusing as it does the language of relationships with computer jargon, it raises a couple of points we need to think seriously about.

The first is how we perceive ourselves, and our relationships with others. In the language of the email, relationship partners are peripherals. Reduced to software, relationships are interchangeable, upgradeable and expendable. Convenience is more important than commitment.

The second point of interest is the way that the email describes people as commodities, and relationships as lifestyle options. Just as our contemporary culture invites us to periodically reinvent our personal image, so it invites us to reinvent our relationships according to short-term personal preference. Of course, the email was just a joke. But it was a joke with a barb because both these factors that it highlights are true of our world today. We have become so used to the production, advertising and consumption of commodities that almost nobody has noticed that we have slipped into treating other people as commodities and measuring our own satisfaction and personhood according to what we possess.

No book on contemporary culture would be complete without some discussion of the role that television plays in our current understanding of ourselves and our environment. Douglas Groothuis goes so far as to call television the 'agent of truth decay' and it isn't hard to see why. On British terrestrial television there are around 125,000 advertising slots a week. It is estimated that most of us view 1,200 advertising images every day. We don't notice most of them, so used have we become to the invasion. Yet if they didn't work, they wouldn't be there.

Some questions

Pause for a moment and consider what answers you would give to the following basic questions:

1. What are we created for?
2. What sort of things does advertising suggest we should seek in life?
3. How much do you think you are personally affected by advertising?

Advertising

Advertising is the oil in the gears of twenty-first century consumerism. It works by two methods. Firstly, it creates a desire that it promises to satisfy but never does. Advertising works a little like addiction, promising much but delivering only an increased desire for more. Secondly, over the years, it creates a whole cultural milieu, made up of new genres of literature (the commercial that tells a whole story in thirty seconds is fast becoming the dominant literary mode of the new century), an overwhelming flood of images and an expectation of personal value and identity based on products. The part that television plays in this cannot be overstated. There is no doubt that most people consider television as their greatest source of information about the world and their greatest source of stimulation and thought-provocation about themselves. We take our signals about the world extensively from TV.

We increasingly depend on the content of television programmes to teach us. We tune in to documentaries or news broadcasts for reliable comment on what we should think and believe, for the current affairs that should concern or excite us. As we do this, we also reinforce in ourselves unconscious assumptions about the reliability of what we are watching. These assumptions are based on nothing more concrete than the authority that television claims for itself. 'If it is important enough to be on the telly,' we reason, 'then it must be valuable or true.'

In one sense we must concur with Baudrillard that truth or falsity is very hard to establish from television. The factor most responsible for the blurring of fact and fiction is that someone is setting the agenda for television programmes without telling us what that agenda is. In addition, fewer and fewer large producers are providing more and more content. What is at stake is nothing less than the domination of culture. But to what end? I want to suggest that the current trend in TV spin-offs, cross-promotions, merchandising and product placement demonstrates a clearly commercial agenda. Our personal and cultural lives are subtly manipulated, through the medium of television, to make us buy. Sales of Red Stripe Beer famously went up by fifty-three per cent after Tom Cruise sipped it in *The Firm*. We should hardly be surprised to hear of multi-million pound link-ups between television and film producers on the one hand and people who produce and market products on the other. Columbia Pictures, for example, was a subsidiary of Coca Cola from 1982–89. Groothuis comments that 'Television is an unreality appliance that dominates our mentality.'[7] We should ask: who exactly is doing the dominating and to what end?

In fairness, clearly not all television producers deliberately produce programmes to a commercial agenda (other than the need to provide good television, which is a commercial agenda in its own right). But as H. R. Rookmaaker comments:

> programme makers are compelled to follow the latest trends and insights and ideas, often without any attempt to come to grips with their underlying principles.[8]

Or, in other words, the pressure to keep up with what is new, exciting and marketable means that programmers produce material that inadvertently reflects cultural trends. They can do so simply from pressure to perform rather than because they think about or understand the engines that are driving contemporary culture. Rookmaaker continues:

> So modern views are constantly preached in a most effective way: effective because it is not intended or overt, so we are not on our guard against it. The message is there, from pop music up to the most sophisticated 'cultural' programme and the most intellectual lecture.

There it is. The medium of television is driven by agendas to shape our thinking, our buying habits and our lives – and now the same is also true of the internet. I do not want to suggest that we should never enjoy television, nor that we should retreat from our culture, as if that were even possible. We should rejoice that Christians with conviction and integrity can and do serve Christ in the television industry, but we must also recognize the dangers inherent in the medium. These dangers are not simply at the level of content but at the level of television itself.

The medium is not value neutral. It is deeply Postmodern in its content, in its form – the smorgasbord of shots, camera angles and short attention spans – and in its self-referentiality. TV has become *the* defining cultural artefact. The number of soap actors who are asked for their opinions on every matter of life and belief, as if their characters were real, powerfully demonstrates this fact. Many similarly see programmes like *The Simpsons* as the ultimate showcase comment on American life. People look to *Ally McBeal* or *Friends* not only to see their own attitudes, neuroses and approaches to relationships reflected there, but to find their own definitions and ideals of what life should be like. At one point the UK show *Yes, Minister*, about the life of a fictional cabinet minister, became so popular that it was seriously suggested that the actor Paul Eddington should run for Parliament. Life is genuinely mirroring art.

The Simpsons is particularly interesting in this regard because of the speed with which many of its words, phrases and attitudes have entered the lexicon. At the mention of Homer people think not about the Greek playwright but the cartoon. And with lavish Postmodern irony the cartoon *knows* it is a cartoon! Real-life actors sign up to play cartoon versions of themselves in the show, strongly increasing the engagement between the cartoon and American life and also simultaneously undermining any sense of living a life unmediated by television.

Television is not neutral. Even public service broadcasting is driven by what will make good television rather than by any consistent set of values or by the noble vision of a Lord Reith. The effect is to cause us to see life through the eyes of television, letting it shape our decisions, attitudes and values. We make decisions according to what we feel is important. Television claims for itself the ability to inform us of what is important.

The decisions that we make, the values that we act upon, and the way we evaluate ourselves and the world are crucial factors, however, in shaping the people and the society that we become. Identity has become one of the defining themes of the early twenty-first century. We are searching for authenticity and value. For many, life is a quest of discovery about who we really are. The influential newspaper columnist Bernard Levin summed this up when he said: 'Have I time to discover why I was born before I die? … Because I am unable to believe it was an accident and if it wasn't one it must have a meaning.'

It is deeply ironic that the one medium that we allow most control over our decisions and our personal identity – television – is the one medium that is wholly unreliable in helping us reach truthful and thoughtful conclusions. The only answers television offers are conclusions about the sort of people advertisers would like us to be. The things television considers most important and newsworthy are the scandalous and the provocative, or items of lowest common denominator, such as sex and money. The British Channel 5 is a perfect example. Combining low production values with much mild titillation, it demonstrates just how poor content can be as long as viewers support the advertising.

Which promise of happiness will we trust?

The Old Testament book of Hosea is a devastating critique of the national life of Israel in Hosea's day. God's people have run after idols in the hope that these idols will make them fruitful, prosperous and happy. They have taken the entire blessing that God has given them and lavished it on foreign nations and foreign gods, thinking that somehow they are more reliable and trustworthy than Yahweh.

In the most graphic and distressing terms the book of Hosea describes this as spiritual prostitution. God instructs Hosea to take a prostitute as his wife:

> When the LORD began to speak through Hosea, the LORD said to him, 'Go, take to yourself an adulterous

> wife and children of unfaithfulness, because the land is guilty of the vilest adultery in departing from the LORD.'
>
> Hosea 1:2

The marriage of Hosea to Gomer visually acts out the relationship between God and Israel. Time and time again she is unfaithful to Hosea, just as Israel is repeatedly unfaithful to Yahweh. Hosea's heart is broken, just as Yahweh's heart is broken. Every time someone asks Hosea what he is doing marrying an unfaithful wife, he is to reply that this is how God feels about Israel. Every time Hosea is cuckolded and shamed, he is to proclaim that this is how Israel is behaving towards God. It is a shocking and visceral illustration.

Perhaps the most shocking part of the story of Hosea and Gomer is how Israel has taken all God's blessings and used them to buy the favour of other nations. In this sense she is worse than a prostitute because she pays for the pleasure of prostituting herself. The sadness is that, just like Hosea with Gomer, God has lavished love on Israel, given her everything she needs. Indeed, he has given himself to her in marriage. Every good thing that Israel could possibly desire was hers in her covenant marriage relationship with God. She had every possibility for delight and happiness. All this she threw away because the world seemed to offer more. The leaders of Israel turn away from knowing God and deliberately ignore him instead:

> my people are destroyed from lack of knowledge. Because you have rejected knowledge, I also reject you as my priests; because you have ignored the law of your God, I also will ignore your children. The more the priests increased, the more they sinned against me; they exchanged their Glory for something disgraceful.
>
> Hosea 4:6–7

This verse is picked up by the apostle Paul in Romans 1, where he tells us that mankind as a whole, though knowing God, does not glorify him (verse 21), deliberately chooses not to retain the knowledge of God (28) and suppresses the truth by wickedness (18). All this has the inevitable result that God withdraws his presence and his blessing, giving people over to the consequences of their sinfulness. Consider carefully the words of Romans 1:28:

> Furthermore, since they did not think it worth while to retain the knowledge of God, he gave them over to a depraved mind ...

People have made, and continue to make, value judgments on what is worthwhile. We don't think God is worth the bother. Romans 1 tells us that all people are like Gomer, the unfaithful wife. She decided that marriage on a human level was not as worthwhile as pursuing lovers. Paul tells us that the picture is true not only of Israel but of all people. We would rather have what the spirit of the age offers than all the pleasure and delight of knowing God. We deliberately turn away from our husband and renounce his blessing.

Glory and delight

We turn away because we have sinful hearts. We would rather believe lies about ourselves than apply God's truth. We do *not* find greater happiness, however, in what the spirit of the age offers than in God. The exact opposite is true. Even a cursory glance through the Psalms shows this to be the case:

> Righteousness and justice are the foundation of your throne; love and faithfulness go before you. Blessed are those who have learned to acclaim you, who walk in the light of your presence, O LORD. They rejoice in your

> name all day long; they exult in your righteousness. For you are their glory and strength, and by your favour you exalt our horn. Indeed, our shield belongs to the LORD, our king to the Holy One of Israel.
>
> Psalm 89:14–18

Does this sound like the words of someone who finds more pleasure in the spirit of the age than in God? Of course not! He has discovered in his walk with the Lord that God is true and just, infinitely loving and faithful, and that walking in his presence brings blessing, rejoicing and delight in righteousness. Why is this? Because God is the Psalmist's glory and strength and he shows him favour in his protection and provision. Or consider this from Psalm 119:

> Oh, how I love your law! I meditate on it all day long. Your commands make me wiser than my enemies, for they are ever with me. I have more insight than all my teachers, for I meditate on your statutes. I have more understanding than the elders, for I obey your precepts. I have kept my feet from every evil path so that I might obey your word. I have not departed from your laws, for you yourself have taught me. How sweet are your words to my taste, sweeter than honey to my mouth! I gain understanding from your precepts; therefore I hate every wrong path.
>
> Psalm 119:97–104

This is not a person who finds his Bible dusty and dry, but a spring of life. Notice the comparatives: God's commands make him *wiser,* they provide *greater* understanding than is available elsewhere, they are *sweeter* than the sweetest thing provided by the spirit of the age, honey. Most importantly perhaps, the commands make him able to avoid wrong paths and to keep his feet from evil. Glorying in God and delighting in his Word is our primary moral responsibility, the only way to walk correctly.

You may think by now that we have wandered off the subject of television. We need to see, however, that the pleasure of God is *greater* than the pleasure of the spirit of the age. TV succeeds in seducing us by holding out promises of happiness. It is subtle and powerful and is capable of telling persuasive lies. It is not that TV is completely incapable of making valuable contributions or transmitting programmes of genuine value and beauty, but when television persuades us to seek all our *identity* and *happiness* in the product that it offers, it has won and we have lost, because then we do not seek it in our God.

Normal Christian living

We need to avoid overly demonizing TV. The medium was, after all, not invented to perpetuate wickedness and the technology itself is neutral. We do need to be aware, however, that it is a deeply flawed way of applying truth to our lives. Television is not about truth; it is about entertainment. It does not aim to reveal true things about us nor to help us to understand who we are in God. It majors in fiction rather than reality, and escapism rather than truth. Television can therefore so easily be the world of Gomer's lovers – promising much in the way of satisfaction in life but providing nothing. Indeed, less than nothing. Just as Israel was so seduced by the nations that she paid for their love, so television is designed to get us to pay for the happiness it claims to offer.

Television's promise of happiness is ephemeral and capricious. It tells us that we have a right to be happy and that being happy means being entertained. Of course, this is just commodification – entertainment is the means by which someone can package happiness and sell it to us. We can be happy as long as we buy into the image. God's promise of happiness, however, is complete in him, because what he offers is just that – himself. It is marriage with our Maker that lasts forever in perfect delight; a relationship for which we were created and without which we are forever incomplete. He is a perfect sustainer and provider; in the Psalmist's words, our glory and strength. The truth is that television seems to promise a lot but in fact gets us to settle for far too little. Sadly, Christians often seem to just live by the spirit of the age, meandering to church on Sunday for meaningless services, occasionally reading the Bible but not discovering in it the source of life and joy that the Psalmist knew, making the Christian life a matter of duty rather than finding in Jesus our delight.

How at odds this is with a biblical understanding of who we are! Consider Paul's words in Colossians. Speaking of Christ he says:

> He is the image of the invisible God, the firstborn over all creation. For by him all things were created: things in heaven and on earth, visible and invisible, whether thrones or powers or rulers or authorities; all things were created by him and for him. He is before all things, and in him all things hold together. And he is the head of the body, the church; he is the beginning and the firstborn from among the dead, so that in everything he might have the supremacy. For God was pleased to have all his fulness dwell in him, and through him to reconcile to himself all things, whether things on earth or things in heaven, by making peace through his blood, shed on the cross.
>
> Colossians 1:15–20

Jesus created all things, and all things were created for him. This includes us as the highpoint of God's creation. We are made for him, for his pleasure, for his purposes. This is a long way from the slot-machine idea of a God who exists to satisfy our whims. Rather, we discover our identity most fully and finally in coming to know that we are created by and for Christ. We also discover our purpose in life in Christ, because it is in him that all things hold together. If you are living with a world-view that doesn't include the supremacy of Jesus in all things, then you are in flat contradiction of what God says in his Word. Only in Jesus do we find the fullness of God; only in him do we discover reconciliation with God. Only at the cross do we find forgiveness of sin and eternal life in Christ.

The supremacy of Jesus explains, therefore, why we exist. Colossians is clear – we exist for Jesus and because of Jesus. We find our purpose and fulfilment in Jesus; we know forgiveness and peace with God through him. If our understanding and experience of the Christian life is anything less than this, then we have been sold a dud. Our identity is in Jesus. The experience of Colossians is normal Christian living.

Television and truth

The apostle John wrote:

> This is the message we have heard from him and declare to you: God is light; in him there is no darkness at all. If we claim to have fellowship with him yet walk in the darkness, we lie and do not live by the truth. But if we walk in the light, as he is in the light, we have fellowship with one another, and the blood of Jesus, his Son, purifies us from all sin.
>
> 1 John 1:5–7

His challenge is that we should live in the light and not in the darkness. John says this is closely connected to living by the truth. The original recipients of his letter were facing subtle heresy that would eventually develop into what came to be called Gnosticism. At the heart of Gnosticism was the idea that real spirituality comes with secret insider spiritual knowledge. So throughout his letter the apostle repeatedly appeals to his readers to stick firmly to the gospel that they have received and to reject anything else: 'See that what you have heard from the beginning remains in you. If it does, you also will remain in the Son and in the Father. And this is what he promised us – even eternal life' (1 John 2:24–25).

We are to remain in Jesus and test everything to make sure we do not swallow lies. Anything else is a rejection of the truth by those who would like to lead Christians astray. The letter is full of hints and tips for testing and discerning:

> Dear friends, do not believe every spirit, but test the spirits to see whether they are from God, because many false prophets have gone out into the world. This is how you can recognise the Spirit of God: Every spirit that acknowledges that Jesus Christ has come in the flesh is from God, but every spirit that does not acknowledge Jesus is not from God. This is the spirit of the antichrist, which you have heard is coming and even now is already in the world.
>
> You, dear children, are from God and have overcome them, because the one who is in you is greater than the one who is in the world. They are from the world and therefore speak from the viewpoint of the world, and the world listens to them. We are from God, and whoever knows God listens to us; but whoever is not from God does not listen to us. This is how we recognise the Spirit of truth and the spirit of falsehood.
>
> 1 John 4:1–6

We test spirits and discern the work of false spirits from that of the Holy Spirit by their testimony to Jesus. John knew that there were powerful spiritual forces at play in the world that like to take falsehood and pass it off as truth.

It may be stretching the point a little far from this passage to say that the same is true for television. But nevertheless we have seen that TV is a medium that makes truth claims for itself whilst powerfully broadcasting the values of the spirit of the age. Not only so, but it also tends to quash debate on truth, replacing it instead with image. Much has been written on the TV presidential debates between Richard Nixon and John F. Kennedy, with most commentators firmly of the opinion that the results of that key American election were determined not by policy but by image. The same thing might be said about recent elections in the UK. The television spin industry is at the heart of national life. Douglas Groothuis says: 'when image dominates the word, rational discourse ends.'[9]

Christians believe that truth is most reliably communicated through a combination of events and the reliable explanation of those events. This is most powerfully true of Scripture. The Bible is the record of God's actions in history, along with God's own explanation of those actions. But the same criteria are applicable to any truthful communication. Television is brilliant at presenting event and fatally compromised at presenting explanation. We have no relationship with the presenter through which we might be able to know how reliable or trustworthy they are. We have no inside knowledge of the editorial policies that dictate which stories are shown and for what reason. Rather, we sit on the receiving end of an implicit agenda that is often hard to discern.

In the absence of reliability TV gets by through apparently transmitting unmediated image and allowing viewers to make up their minds. Of course, the image is not unmediated and there is much to help the viewer come to the 'correct' conclusion. But Groothuis' point is undeniable – image dominates the word and forecloses rational discourse. It is this that makes television the ultimate Postmodern medium – it is deeply significant in communicating the Postmodern values of society and constructing images and identity without foundations.

One of the most powerful ways that TV takes contemporary cultural theories and values and turns them into public opinion is the talk show that involves the audience. Oprah Winfrey is possibly the most powerful opinion-former on the planet. What Oprah thinks today, America thinks tomorrow; what Trisha or Kilroy allow on their show today is the conversation point of tomorrow. A recent episode of Trisha had a young man pleading with his brother and girlfriend to turn their backs on the pornography industry. They were unrepentant. Trisha was in a quandary. Her sympathies were clearly with the young man but there was no way she was about to tell the couple they were wrong. She ended by wishing them well in whatever they wanted to do and half-heartedly thanking the young guest for his concern. 'If it feels good, then do it!' was the powerful message of the programme. 'Don't let anyone else challenge your right to do anything at all.'

These sorts of values get transmitted back into the public arena through TV phone-ins, polls of public opinion on breakfast television and, of course, advertising. Through these mechanisms TV presents itself as democracy in action. And who would want to disagree with democracy? This is partly why we have given such status to Oprah-type figures. They are held up as the bastions of free-thinking democratic right to reply. This couldn't be further from the truth. Instead they are creating their own dumbed-down versions of reality and inviting the mass-consumer to participate. I say 'dumbed-down' because, as David Wells helpfully puts it:

> if [TV] can make Oprah more real and personable than one's next door neighbour, it can do something comparable with the tragedies and desolations of life as well. Television takes the experience of the world and filters it into our living room in digestible, commercially convenient chunks ...[10]

More questions

What then are we to do with the apostle John's exhortation to discern truth from falsehood? Pause for a minute and consider your responses to these questions:

1. How important is TV in forming your opinions about the world?
2. Do you try to be discerning when you watch TV?
3. If so, by what means do you try to test truth and falsehood? If not, how could you teach yourself to be more discerning?

The essential answer to such questions lies in submitting ourselves, and all our opinions, to God. We must allow him to dictate on matters of truth and falsehood. After all, he is the one who reveals himself as the Truth. When Jesus claims to be the Way, the Truth and the Life in John 14:6, he is not claiming to be *a* truth, one among many, but to embody in himself the very nature of truth. If we want to know the truth we look to Jesus, measure everything else by him and then submit ourselves and our lives to him. This is what James exhorts us to do in a very pertinent passage:

> What causes fights and quarrels among you? Don't they come from your desires that battle within you? You want something but don't get it. You kill and covet, but you cannot have what you want. You quarrel and fight. You do not have, because you do not ask God. When you ask, you do not receive, because you ask with wrong motives, that you may spend what you get on your pleasures.
>
> You adulterous people, don't you know that friendship with the world is hatred towards God? Anyone who chooses to be a friend of the world becomes an enemy of God. Or do you think Scripture says without reason that the spirit he caused to live in us envies intensely? But he gives us more grace. That is why Scripture says: 'God opposes the proud but gives grace to the humble.'
>
> Submit yourselves, then, to God. Resist the devil, and he will flee from you. Come near to God and he will come near to you.
>
> James 4:1–8

Notice what James is saying here. It seems that Christians are falling out because of their covetousness. They are pursuing material things at the expense of each other, quarrelling, fighting, maybe even killing! It is devastating their prayer lives because they treat God simply as the source of material things. They fall into the twin traps of either not praying at all or praying with totally twisted motives. What a dreadful state! The punch is in verse 4 where James says that this is spiritual adultery (remember Hosea and Gomer?), friendship with the world and hatred towards God. He says that we become friends with the world by choosing to be, and that when we so choose we enflame the holy jealousy of the Spirit of God.

What is the answer? Submitting ourselves to God.

Deliberately aligning ourselves with the truth and turning from the spirit of the age. Coming near to God and distancing ourselves from the world. This does not mean hermetically sealing ourselves off in a monastery, but, rather, applying God's values to ourselves, our lives and our viewing habits. It means taking the gospel and living it when we are in front of the TV. James tells us that God is interested in our television viewing because he is interested in our hearts. He is interested in what we allow inside our heads because he is jealous for our affections, as jealous as a husband for the love of his wife.

Responding to truth means rejecting false and fake ideas of reality. It has become deeply unfashionable in the church in recent years to stand up against falsehood. We fear looking intolerant. But Postmodernism and the Postmodern media trade in falsity. If we are reluctant to stand on the gospel in such a climate, we must ask ourselves whether we really believe the gospel. Watching TV is a moral exercise that we do before a God of moral purity. Discerning truth from falsehood is just as much a moral exercise because Jesus is the Truth. Jesus defines reality. Jesus determines what is valuable and what is worthless in this world. Jesus is the only place to find true identity in a channel-surfing world. But Jesus is not entertainment and we must never let the assumptions of the entertainment industry persuade us to present the gospel as mere fun or one option among many. To do so is to degrade the Maker of the universe.

Finally, advertising works best in communities that have no way of defining people or society morally. Advertising is by and large anti-truth and pro-acquisition. But we only correctly understand ourselves morally with respect to the good news of Jesus. Our media poses the big question for Christians. Are we sold as slaves to the values of the age, which tell us to accumulate because this life is all we get, or do we think and act in accordance with God's truth as he has revealed it in the Bible, proclaiming Jesus to a Postmodern world? If the latter, then we will enjoy television, but we will do so with a Christian critique. For surely the challenge of our contemporary culture is not to stick our heads in the sand, dump the TV and withdraw from cultural debate, but to train ourselves and our children to engage critically with our world and its values and the way that television presents them. TV is not about to go away, and many Christians labour hard for Christ in the media world. We need to watch with integrity, delighting in transmissions that would delight God, earnestly interacting with intelligent fiction and discussion about the world and about ourselves, and challenging ourselves and others when TV plummets into the gutter.

Chapter 11

Conclusions: Proclaiming the Authentic Jesus

A gospel under attack

It is my belief that the gospel of Jesus Christ is strongly and consciously under attack from all that goes under the heading *Postmodernism*. This assault comes through both contemporary theory and post-Christian culture. Culture is a diverse and varied thing. While the core of Postmodernism is relativism, pluralism and the suspicion of truth, its outworkings are manifold and the form it takes varies from situation to situation. The main challenge of Modernism was to God's very existence. Postmodernism has replaced the few heavy hammer-blows of Modernism – such as scientific materialism – with a wide variety of assaults of much greater subtlety. The challenge to the existence of God has been replaced with challenges to the uniqueness of Jesus. It is rare today to hear impassioned argument from non-Christians that we should not believe in God. It is much more common to hear arguments such as: 'Christianity is fine for you; I'm glad it works for you. But you have your way and I have mine. Isn't it enough for you that I am happy?'

This line of reasoning, of course, depends entirely on there being nothing that is true for all people. Postmodernism underlines this denial at every point. Happiness is held up as the ultimate good but never fleshed out or explored. How happy do we have to be? And for how long? What if a lie can make us happy while the truth can unnerve and upset us – does this mean that happiness is more important than reality? If so, we will always look to escape from the harsh realities of the world into comfortable and safe fantasies. We will always replace long-term or eternal good with short-term anaesthetics, and replace short-term harsh realities with the drugs of materialism and self-satisfaction.

Most importantly, this view challenges the fact that Jesus Christ is unique. It tells us that we don't have to live for him in order to enjoy the highest good or to escape judgment. We can live however we like, expecting no judgment from the God we deny. We can live according to any moral values, or none. We can believe anything we like, and it is good because we believe it. We expect that if there is a God he will accept our self-defined standards of goodness that always tell us we are right. We may never tell anyone else that they are wrong. This is now the only genuine offence left in our society.

To this culture the good news of Jesus comes as a profound shock. Here we find a man who claims to be God, and to be the *only* way to be reconciled to God. He tells us that, far from fashioning reality in our own image to our own comfort, we are guests of his reality, and our ultimate good, for now and forever, is only to be found with him. And the flip side of the good news is bad news. Unless we accept this Christ, his dire warning is that we will spend eternity without God in eternal, conscious punishment for our presumption. Far from being unfair or tyrannical, this is considered a completely just response from a pure, holy Creator to unholy rebels. The real shock, however, is not that God punishes, but that he provides any way out at all. The unfairness is not that he doesn't rescue everyone, regardless of their deeds, but that he rescues anyone, in spite of our rebellion.

Postmodernism has turned the offence of the gospel upside down. It says that Christians are offensive in proclaiming only one way of salvation. The reality of the situation is that we should be offended that there is *any* way of salvation. We should be offended by the cross, offended by our sin and guilt, and then immensely grateful, from the depths of our souls, for such a great and magnificent Saviour.

We shall never offend the world with the salvation of God, never confront it with the cross of Jesus, unless we are convinced of his uniqueness. The Postmodern destruction of authority is, above all, a challenge to uniqueness. We shall completely fail to meet *the* challenge of our times unless we are convinced about the uniqueness of the Jesus of the Bible, and proclaim him to everyone. This will involve us not only in presenting positive evidence from Scripture and from transformed lives that Jesus lives and reigns, but also in refuting error. Even where truth remains a popular concept, the whole idea that therefore we must refute error is often unthinkable. But truth always and unfailingly highlights error, sometimes gently, sometimes openly and strongly. It cannot but do so.

Some questions

Recall that we have seen that the three pillars of Postmodernism are relativism, pluralism and the distrust of metanarratives. Then consider:

1. How do each of these pillars challenge Jesus' unique right to our obedience?
2. What do each of these pillars say about Jesus' Godship and authority?
3. How does understanding Jesus' uniqueness challenge the pillars of Postmodernism?
4. Why is it vital to be secure about the uniqueness of Jesus?

The uniqueness of Jesus

Relativism tells me that I am the centre of all things, that the world is here to fulfil me and finds its meaning in relation to me. The world is shaped around the satisfaction of self. But Jesus is God. He made everything, he knows all things and he reveals himself accurately. He commands and deserves obedience. At the core of what he reveals is the shocking fact that what needs satisfying is not our felt needs, but God's just demand that sin is paid for, either by our death or by Jesus' death on our behalf. (See the Afterword to this chapter.) Only here is God satisfied, only here can we be reconciled with him and glorified in Jesus.

Pluralism in its Postmodern form challenges the gospel at just this point. It tells us that to claim that there is only one way is intolerably offensive to those who do not wish it to be so. With the best will in the world, this only works if you deny truthfulness and allow that people can believe *anything*, and must be applauded and valued for their beliefs. It only works if there are not many ways to God, but none. If all are equally lost, then we should all be respectful pluralists. Pluralism claims to dignify all belief but actually dignifies none. It heralds that all positions are important and valuable, but only works if none of them are actually true. It arrogantly claims to be able to judge all positions to be equal, and to stand in judgment over those who disagree.

And pluralism is wrong. We must certainly value other

races and other cultural heritages. But beliefs outside the gospel do not show that people seek God; rather that they rebel against his true revelation of himself. Alternative gospels demonstrate not spirituality but idolatry; not saintliness but wilful sin. Romans 1 is a dreadful portrayal of the pluralist world. It tells us that people deliberately suppress the plain truth in their wickedness (verse 18), that we knew God but refused to glorify him or give him thanks (21) and that we did not consider it worthwhile to retain knowledge of him (28). This is not helpful, pluralist religion. It is a shameful shaking of our fists in the face of the Creator. God's response is not to congratulate us on creative and life-affirming religion; it is to give people over to the consequences of wickedness, and to rightly reveal his wrath against us.

Jesus says that he is the Way, the Truth and the Life (John 14:6). The pluralist starts with the assumption that we are basically good and therefore deserve God's favour. For God to judge is then unfair in the face of our goodness. The biblical Christian starts from the understanding that, despite being made in God's image and having many wonderful characteristics, we are all rebels deserving judgment. For God to judge is right, and for God to rescue is our deepest need. At the heart of pluralism is a totally unChristian understanding of human nature.

For there *is* a metanarrative at work in this universe. God is working to have a people for himself, saved by the death of Jesus. He will dwell with them for all eternity when he wraps up this creation and completes a new one. All Christians yearn for this (Revelation 22:17). It will be the day to end all days. The metanarrative is vital. If we misunderstand this then we are, literally, doomed.

Proclaiming the unique Christ

It is therefore critical that, as thinking Christians and

churches, we learn to proclaim the gospel faithfully to our culture. We must not get it wrong, because eternity is at stake for lost people. We can hope and pray for changes in our culture so that issues of truth come to be more kindly regarded once again, but our main motivation is not to change the culture but to change lives. We long to see the Lord rescue lost people as the good news of Jesus is told to all.

I hope that this book has provided some help to understand our culture, and has prompted you to think about how you can bring the good news to your peers in culturally friendly ways. Yet if we are to take up the vital challenge of understanding our culture, how much more must we learn to understand the gospel and get to know our God. It is no good for us to spend all our time and energy on things that are purely of this world at the expense of the things of God. This world will pass away. In a billion years' time much that we value now will seem very inconsequential. But Jesus and his words will never pass away. We need to value the gospel above all.

I suggest that there are four key areas that we should major on if we are to strongly engage our culture and the anti-Christian ideas that lie behind it. These are: (1) developing robust godliness; (2) squarely facing the facts about the current situation; (3) understanding underlying ideas in order to critically engage with them and stand up against them; and (4) challenging our own comfortable sub-culture.

Developing robust godliness

By 'robust godliness' I mean the sort of devotion to Christ that not only is wholly committed to Christian living, but is also committed to working out what it means to be a Christian in a hostile setting – committed, in fact, to being a missionary. At the very least we want be Christian disciples who are clear on the gospel in our own minds; who are able to explain it and argue the case for it against opposing world-views; who are able to see points at which our *personal* environment is saying things that are opposed to the gospel; and who are able and unafraid to challenge at that point.

This may sound old hat – after all, we have always wanted to be disciples like this. But honestly, how many of our training programmes and church services regularly get people to this point? My experience is that we often divorce teaching the gospel from teaching about the world around us, or vice versa. As a result we have produced Christians who are clear in the gospel in their minds, and who know some things about contemporary culture, but are unable to apply the one to the other in a coherent, thoughtful way. This happens when we fail to see that the gospel is meant to challenge *our* culture. John Stott uses the phrase 'double listening' to explain the process of listening to the Word and the world, Bible in one hand and newspaper in the other, with the aim of applying the Word *to* the world.

How can we better do double listening? A chapter like this can only, of course, skim the surface. You will have as many good ideas as me, or more. However, the following two things need to characterize all our planning and programmes: a strong emphasis on discipleship, and teaching Christians to evangelize at the level of world-view.

A strong emphasis on discipleship

A colleague of mine defines success in discipling someone as 'the point at which they become self-starters, are able to pass on what they have learnt, and are applying it to their own situation.' He makes this aim clear at the start of any training programme. By the end of the training the trainees will themselves be passing on their learning to others. If they do not do so they haven't learnt anything about being a disciple.

It often feels as though busy Christians and Christian ministers have little time to commit, week after week, to fulfilling a vision like this. Instead we tend to preach or listen to a variety of unconnected sermons or training sessions. My contention is that while the unconnected sermon may have great value as a one-off, this model of teaching the Bible rarely produces strong disciples because it teaches in an unconnected fashion. It does not invest value incrementally, week by week, into our lives. Jesus, however, lived with his disciples for three years. Everything he did and said became material for their growth. Their training was continuous and consisted of learning *and* doing, always under the watchful eye of Christ. There was little distinction to be made between his discipleship programme for them and life itself. Everything became an opportunity to learn how to take the good news of the kingdom and apply it to the world. Recently a student friend said to me, 'I have realized that there is no such thing as an evangelistic opportunity – all of life is to be evangelistic. I am to learn to honour Christ and speak of him in absolutely every situation.'

Evangelizing at the level of world-view

I am grateful to Professor Don Carson for this idea, which I think is increasingly critical. His point is that we live in a culture with few or no Christian presuppositions, but we often think that it does have such presuppositions. People don't even know basic Bible stories any more, let alone understand biblical concepts vital to successful engagement with the gospel, such as sin, the need for redemption, heaven and hell, or even God. Furthermore, where they do know something about Christian ideas, they have frequently written them off as archaic or even unethical.

In this situation it is no good simply proclaiming that

Jesus saves people, because people haven't understood why they need to be saved, or from what. In other words, they need to understand the gospel in the light of the story-line of the whole Bible. They need to know the problems raised by the Old Testament in order to understand the answers that the New Testament gives, and the place of Jesus in those answers.

A generation ago we might have had grounds for bypassing the Bible's story-line and going straight to Jesus. Carson maintains, and I agree, that this is increasingly likely to fail. He takes the example of Paul in Athens in Acts 17, showing that Paul engages the pluralistic culture of Athens at the level of their world-view, their assumptions about the world. This was a vital part of Paul's strategy, because he was not simply proclaiming Christ into a vacuum, but was engaging people with a highly developed *opposing* world-view. The Athenians had all sorts of presuppositions that they were not going to give up lightly. Postmoderns have all sorts of presuppositions that they are not going to give up lightly either. An over-simplistic presentation to people who consider themselves sophisticated in the area of ideas will not work. We must present the whole plot in order to show that they have a defective world-view from the start.

Hence Paul begins by proclaiming God's activity in creation, his sovereignty, his sufficiency and a host of other things before he gets to Christ and the resurrection. He knew from the start that the proclamation of Jesus was his goal, but he dealt convincingly with religious and philosophical obstacles to the gospel first, by telling the Bible's plot-line. His aim was to show that the Bible offered a better and more plausible account of the world than the Athenians could. By the time Paul proclaims Christ they have seen the need for something that answers the problems the Bible has raised.

We are no longer in a culture in which we can assume that people understand Christian concepts, have a Christian background or respond to Christian jargon. We are once again in an Athenian situation, and we must understand and proclaim the whole message, or be left with an emasculated and misunderstood message.

A unified training programme?

These two things – strong discipleship and learning to evangelize at the level of world-view – need to characterize our teaching and training. Why do we offer training on understanding the spirit of the age and something entirely different on understanding the Bible? Why shouldn't we do both at once? Certainly, a keen grasp of the plot-line of the Bible is more likely to make people wonder at such a salvation – and more fired to proclaim it! Below is an outline of a suggested brief training course that would work in a local church or a university Christian Union:

A brief course in Bible and culture

Weeks 1–4. Understanding the Bible: Bible overview.

Weeks 5–9. Understanding the culture: specific Postmodern challenges – possibly using Part 1 of this book, encouraging people to understand their social situations from a gospel perspective.

Week 10. Key concepts to uphold in a Postmodern world: revelation, authority, the uniqueness of Christ, humanity, community.

Week 11. Why the gospel presents better answers than those offered by our culture and how to graciously confront error.

Week 12. How trainees can train others in understanding the Bible and culture.

Note that I am not suggesting that *all* teaching and training should have the twin themes of Bible and culture over an extended period, but that there is much value in a short course, perhaps especially for university and higher education students and those who minister to them. Students often feel as though they have two options, both of which are inadequate. They can either be keen to learn from their lecturers and get progressively weaker on the gospel, or be strong on the gospel but not open to learn.

By teaching the gospel in a way that highlights the differences between the truth and the teaching that students receive at college or university, we shall train them to engage rather than to entrench. By teaching all Christians to discern where our culture is at odds with the message of Jesus, we will produce robust witness in a hostile world.

Squarely facing the facts

Many Christians are immersed daily in an environment that is toxic to our faith. This is the case socially, at work and, for Christian students, at college. Many of us, however, have only the dimmest awareness that this is the case or why it should be so. We need to help develop evaluative and critical skills, in order that we may understand, and withstand, our environment. How may we do this?

Christians need help in evaluating their own thinking

The following questions may help you think about whether you approach life Christianly:

1. What assumptions do you make about the world? Do you assume people are fundamentally good or bad? Do you understand how to distinguish good from evil by biblical principles?
2. To what extent do you think your friends consciously or subconsciously buy into the non-Christian assump-

tions of the world around them? Now ask the same question of yourself.
3. How good is your Bible knowledge?
4. Do you understand why it is vital for you to apply biblical understanding, values and principles to your life, work and study?
5. What particular aspects of contemporary culture and society are most likely to challenge your faith?
6. Do you ever think about the way culture influences you, either positively or negatively?
7. Are you able to clearly explain your faith to non-Christians?
8. Do you ever pause to reflect on whether you are growing in your faith?

Asking ourselves questions such as these helps us to face the facts about ourselves and our situations. Our hope is to be further on in our journey with God in a year's time than we are now. Sadly, many of us simply tread water in our Christian lives because we have no desire to grow. The result is slow stagnation and the atrophy of our spiritual muscle.

It is well worth setting ourselves some targets for spiritual growth, and growth in our Christian thinking. A student, for example, might decide that he wishes to understand why a feminist lecturer thinks the way she does, and to develop some understanding of a biblical response during the next term. A Christian shopkeeper might decide to dedicate some time each week to thinking about what it means to be a good steward of money and resources. A company director might set herself some targets about learning how to manage staff Christianly. We live in a society that enjoys setting targets in almost every area. There is a passion for improvement and excellence. Should not we too strive for improvement and excellence, desiring to know God better and to share him more effectively with others?

Be specific about our learning

Much Christian growth fails to happen because we do not plan to grow. We limit our Christian stimulation to twenty-five-minute Sunday sermons. These can sometimes be random in content and they do not always pursue a biblical theme or book over more than one talk. It is easy for me to make personal time with God into a similarly random experience of picking favourite purple passages in the Bible and expecting God to enrich me through it. The same is true when thinking about the world. When we think at all, it is often at the level of vague generalizations rather than trying to understand specific aspects of the world in depth. This may lead us to shallow Christian living and unthoughtful evangelism. We fail to understand the questions that the world is posing, because we do not listen to the world.

It is very helpful to take specific questions about life and faith, and work out, in detail, the answers that the Bible gives. Small groups of people considering together how to live as Christians are a particularly good way to encourage us to live excellent Christian lives. Groups allow the sharing of ideas and teach us that we cannot live the Christian life alone. Group discussion is an excellent way to explore issues and come to biblical conclusions about living life Christianly. House groups or cells can also provide mutual support, accountability and prayer.

In your church Bible study group, try starting a meeting not with a biblical text but with a specific aspect of society, such as what society says about sexuality or education or the media. Identify two or three issues that are important for Christians to respond to, and then try to develop such a response from the Bible. Alternatively, why not meet one week to discuss a popular non-Christian book, or an academic text if you are a student.

Whatever we do, we should develop ways to ensure that we don't all struggle along separately. Small-group discussion allows us to receive support, and to pass on what we are learning about the Lord and about the world. Belonging prevents us from labouring for the Lord in a vacuum. Questions can be raised and answered. There is opportunity to build each other up in Christ, in understanding the gospel, in engaging the culture, and in producing strong witness to Jesus.

Understanding in order to engage

Being salt and light

Facing the facts about ourselves and about the spirit of the age is vital. We recognize that we need to understand the world in order to reach the world. But how can Christians take on powerful cultural influences? How can Christian students take on powerful academic machines?

Christians, by definition, are capable of understanding our culture better than anyone else because we have access to God's revealed truth about the way the world works. Yet few deliberately work hard at it. Few Christian undergraduates, for instance, go on to become the best Christian postgraduate students. It is important that we do so. Often our response to a fallen, sinful world seems to be to withdraw to the Christian ghetto and let our society get on with it. Jesus instead encourages us to be salt and light – tasty Christians, flavouring and purifying a rotten world.

Engaging the world as a Christian student

It is worth having a brief section here directed specifically to Christian students. Frequently it is only at master's degree level, or above, that the theoretical foundations of any academic discipline are explored. At undergrad level these foundations are presented as presuppositions. Students are expected to submit to them. Similarly, it is only at further degree level that the academy starts to listen seriously to any critique. If you are a robust Christian student it is important to consider prayerfully whether you might serve the Lord best by taking postgraduate courses and living for him in that challenging environment. If you pastor Christian students, this might be a question you can put to them. There are several realities to consider when we ask undergrads to remain in the university in order to combat anti-Christian presuppositions.

Firstly, they are liable to come under sustained assault. I was regularly called a fascist in an MA class in Postmodernism for doing nothing more than affirming the existence of truth. Hence any Christian postgrad needs good support, prayer and accountability.

Secondly, we may be asking people to take courses in which some study material is inherently anti-Christian. While not always *explicitly* immoral, most contemporary theory denies truth, authority and value. Without support, the danger is that a student's spiritual walk may suffer.

Thirdly, it is vital that those who have learnt in, and survived, the postgrad environment have the opportunity to pass on what they have learnt. We could imagine partnership schemes or small groups where undergrads could ask questions in a safe environment and receive wisdom, academically and pastorally, from those who have gone before. Doing this in the context of a church provides further support and wise leadership.

I don't as yet know of any arena where serious thought has been given to producing a forum for Christian undergrads to discuss many of these issues in the context of a local church. The issues are regularly raised at university missions and other evangelistic events, but then it is usually the case that an 'expert' is wheeled on to speak and take questions. This has two effects. The first is that it reinforces to the Christian student that this is an area for experts and not for them. The second effect is that it doesn't tell the non-Christian that the average Christian student has anything worthwhile to say on the subject.

Christian students have much of value to contribute academically, but often fail to do so for fear of being shamed by bright non-Christian colleagues or academics. Can I make a personal plea that we all help any thoughtful students we know to engage in speaking and writing? The Debating Society, the Student Union newspaper, and lectures where contributions are invited from the floor all provide such opportunities to speak for Christ. There must be many others. Students often need encouragement before admitting to themselves that they have anything worth sharing. Take every opportunity to encourage those who are keen and able to express themselves, to do so in as public a way as possible.

In the public domain there is a real scarcity of material on contemporary student and academic issues. I would like to see a surge of high-quality, medium-length papers and articles being made freely available that might be published in college magazines, and elsewhere, under the name of the Christian Union. Do you know students who can write articles like this? Where are they being published? To whom are they being circulated? Encourage them to publish, even if only amongst friends, and to circulate Christian material as widely as possible.

Challenging a comfortable sub-culture

There is no doubt that churches, Christian student groups and individual Christians can become very comfortable and inward looking. Where this happens, two sets of walls are built. The first wall is starting to think there is no reason to engage our culture, that it is possible to be a comfortable Christian. Church can become a retreat rather than the place for being equipped to win the lost. The second wall that results is that non-Christians are excluded from our churchy sub-culture, a clique that is not concerned about them. Sometimes we say that we are concerned for the lost, or that we desire to make our meetings accessible to the outsider, but our demeanour says otherwise. The songs we sing, the jargon we use, the cliques we form can exclude people. Churches and Christian Unions can become most uninviting places. We easily build walls of alienation. Sadly, where such walls are erected, our evangelistic edge is quickly lost.

Another factor constantly to guard against is how readily contemporary assumptions and apathy slip into church life and the mind-set of Christians. Earlier in the book I mentioned how one CU leader said to me, 'If the Bible says one thing and I strongly feel another, surely all I can really go on is my feelings.' She had fallen into a Postmodern way of thinking without even knowing it. Of course, feelings are very important, but where any individual or group of Christians becomes more feeling-orientated than Word-orientated there is great danger of losing authentic Christianity. This is made very easy by its being the path of least resistance. One feels good travelling this path, and few people are likely to despise you for it.

How then should we challenge a comfortable Christian sub-culture? Ask yourself the following questions about your church. Then try to ask them honestly about yourself.

1. Are there areas that you can see where your church is in danger of cultural compromise? For example is the teaching at church becoming more full of illustrations than it is of the Bible? How often do you receive teaching on great biblical themes such as holiness, grace, sin, heaven and hell?
2. Is there a lack of confidence in the gospel? Can people

in your church simply and clearly explain the good news about Jesus without using jargon? Do they understand how it applies to their everyday lives?

3. Are too many songs taken from a Postmodern perspective? So much of what young Christians believe is actually picked up from songs rather than from the Bible. This frightens me. Many modern songs are clearly influenced more by our culture than by genuine Christianity. In any modern songbook simply look at the number of songs that are all about self. Not all are bad, of course, but the trend is worrying.

4. Are the aims of the church unclear? I heard of one Christian group that had a leadership position called 'the intimacy secretary'. They have misunderstood what it means to be the people of God. Close relationships are good but they are not our *raison d'être*. Can leaders and members clearly vocalize sensible, biblical aims?

5. Is there a lack of concern for outsiders? Are you well taught and led in evangelism? Do leaders model the task to you? Are there opportunities for everyone to have a go, no matter what stage he or she is at?

6. Is there apathy in your church or Christian Union? Perhaps there is a need to work at understanding what it means to be a community of believers with a focused goal. Perhaps too there needs to be a sense of mutual accountability and discipline. Without them the group are very unlikely to live or confess the truth with any great fervour. We need peers to help us go against the flow of contemporary culture.

7. Are there too few bridge-points between your church and the world? Does what you hear from the Bible on Sunday actually help you to live as a Christian on Monday?

There are, of course, many factors that result in churches and Christian student groups becoming inaccessible and unfriendly to outsiders, and visionless within. Where there is no vision, the Bible says, people perish. We go cold spiritually, just as a burning coal, when taken from the fire, slowly loses its light, heat and power. If you cannot answer the question, 'What is the Lord doing in your life and your church?' or 'How are you living for him in your situation?' it might be that you are like that dying ember. You need the encouragement of Christians who will help you understand the Lord's priorities for your life and witness, and who will take you forward in his purposes.

Challenging a powerful culture

Make no mistake, the culture we are attempting to challenge with the gospel has become very powerful. Here is a checklist summary for all those who want to join in the task of changing that culture and help others to do so as well:

1. Be committed to the genuine gospel – or fail to communicate real Christianity.
2. Understand the specific challenges facing us at this point in time – or fail to hear what needs to be confronted.
3. Learn to understand and engage both theory and culture – or fail to make the gospel heard.
4. Set yourself clear, specific aims – or fail to know what you want to achieve.
5. Enable others to do the same – or let the initiative die with you.

We need to approach the many-faceted nature of contemporary theory and culture from many directions, enabling all Christians to use their gifts, their relationships and their opportunities, as God gives us the wisdom and ability. We do so in the supreme confidence that Jesus has all authority in heaven and earth. He has promised to be with us as we work for him in winning the world. He is the Lord of all. He has promised to build his church so that the gates of hell itself won't stand against it. Consider the privilege we have in being invited by Jesus to participate in his mission. The invitation is there not because he needs us to do it, but in order that we might become more like him. Challenging a culture with the gospel, taking the good news to the ends of the earth – this is God's work in God's world. He is faithful and he will do it.

*

Afterword: The uniqueness of Jesus

Unique Sonship

Read John 5:16–27 and then consider these questions that John raises:

1. Where does Jesus' authority come from?
2. What sort of authority does Jesus have?

This passage in John's Gospel makes it clear that Jesus is the Son of God *par excellence*. One aspect of sonship in New Testament culture is that sons do what their fathers did. They follow in their fathers' footsteps, and usually in their craft and social status. John 5 tells us that one reason why Jesus is called the Son of God is that he does *only* and *exactly* what the Father does. So close is the identification between Jesus and the Father, and so clearly does he state it, that the religious authorities want to kill him for equating himself with Yahweh.

There are many unique features we could list about Jesus, such as his virgin birth, his sinless life, his exemplary ministry, and his atoning death. Important as these things are, however, they do not get to the heart of his uniqueness. The crux of the matter is that Jesus is unique because he is the Sovereign, Almighty Creator God made flesh. All the facts about his birth, life, death, resurrection, ascension and eternal rule depend on this. He is able to carry out his ministry because of who he is.

Jesus, for example, is described as forgiving sins (Mark 2:7). The Pharisees ironically and caustically think, 'Who can forgive sins except God alone?' The answer is, 'Nobody.' Nobody can forgive sins except Yahweh – he is the one against whom sin is directed. A miracle like the calming of the storm – a unique event if ever there was one – leaves the disciples with one question in their stunned minds: 'Who *is* this man we have hitched up with?' And the answer in Mark's Gospel is obvious: the one who has authority to still the waves with a word is the one who made the oceans with the word of his mouth. Jesus can carry out this ministry because of who he is.

Some have suggested that Jesus' divinity or his miracles were fiction imposed on him by later writers. This is unthinkable. Jesus is very happy to claim the prerogatives of God for himself in a way that is unimaginable for a strongly monotheistic culture. He accepts Thomas worshipping him as God after the resurrection (John 20:28). He identifies himself in the language of divinity, especially in the great 'I AM' statements in John's Gospel. 'I AM' was the great Old Testament expression of God's name and self. Jesus says, 'I AM the bread of life'; 'I AM the true vine'; 'I AM the good shepherd'; 'Before Abraham was I AM'.

Jesus has unique authority because of his unique personhood. We would be right to think that Jesus also, therefore, has access to unique knowledge.

Unique knowledge

Read John 3:11–13 and then consider some more questions that John raises:

1. Why is Jesus' knowledge unique?
2. What must we do in response to Jesus' words, according to these verses?

We discover in John 3 that Jesus can refute the finest of Pharisee theologians because he has come down from heaven. He is the only one who can speak of the things of heaven, and therefore of reality itself, with authority because he is the only one who has been there. Nicodemus thought he knew a thing or two but he was wrong. Only Jesus speaks authoritatively. This is why Jesus is to be obeyed. His words are *true* because he is God. His revelation of God is perfect.

Unique rescue

Jesus' identity and knowledge are unique. That alone should be reason enough to trust him. However, there is one final reason why we must bow the knee to him, and that is because he is the unique offering for sin. We cannot pay the price ourselves except with judgment and being cut off from God. But the Father gave the Son as an atoning sacrifice for sin. God the Father made Jesus, who knew no sin, *to be* sin for us so that we might become the righteousness of God in him (2 Corinthians 5:21). The Father didn't just make Jesus *carry* sin, but *become* sin. The enormity of this will stagger us for all eternity.

This great transaction means that, in Jesus, God now considers us to be as righteous as he is himself! If this doesn't blow our minds, nothing will. It is deeply humbling. That our God should die to achieve this for us and, furthermore, to adopt us as sons along with Jesus, is the greatest truth in creation and eternity. It is not, however, self-empowering. Far from being able to claim our own merits, we have to come to the foot of the cross, admitting our sin and humbly asking forgiveness.

This is the ultimate denial of the relativism that grips our culture. When Thomas worshipped Jesus as Lord and God, it was not subjective. He wasn't God just for Thomas, for then we can take or leave him as we see fit. He is God over all. Therefore what he reveals is absolutely true. What he commands must be obeyed. He has the right to perfect obedience. We are his by the fact that he made us. Christians are additionally his by the fact that we are bought at the price of his blood.

Appendix 1

A Glossary of Postmodern Culture

This brief list of terms is not intended to be comprehensive. It should provide a few pointers to the meaning of certain terms you will find in this book or elsewhere.

Authenticity

The idea that anything has a kernel of inherent value that is independent of its environment. For example, in the area of literature or art this is seen in the idea of a canon of accepted great works. Postmodernists strongly contend that there is no such thing as authenticity. The value of an artefact therefore stems from the way it is received and used rather than from any internal worth.

Author

Criticism has traditionally held that the important point in a text or discourse is what the author intends to convey. By challenging our ability to communicate, Postmodernists suggest that any such intention is not available to us. Hence we should not ask, 'What does this text mean?' but 'What does this text mean to me?' The term 'the death of the author' describes this idea.

Authority

The ability of an author to make definitive and meaningful statements that must be accepted.

Canon
An accepted body of work considered to be authoritative.

Death of the Author
See 'Author' above.

Deconstruction
A tool developed by Jacques Derrida to try to show that it is impossible to determine meaning in a text.

Epistemology
The study of how it is possible to know things. Postmodernists maintain that epistemology is redundant, and that we cannot know anything with certainty. They try to construct a world in which knowing is less important than, and unconnected with, being.

Ethics
A big Postmodern buzz word. Where morality spoke in terms of right and wrong, good and bad, Postmodernists claim that these categories are both obsolete and repressive. They use the word 'ethics' much more broadly to mean the way we deal with other people. They attempt to construct systems of ethics that do not depend on ideas of right and wrong.

Feminism
The theory and movement that tries to correct perceived oppression of women by men.

Gender theory
Closely connected to feminism, gender theory that suggests that issues of gender need to be re-examined. Usually strongly pro-homosexual, often deliberately against accepted norms in relationships, such as marriage.

Generation X
A phrase popularized by Douglas Coupland to describe the generation born between 1960 and 1980. The term designates a generation characterized by apathy, disillusionment and hopelessness.

High Culture
and Low/Pop/Mass Culture. The attempt to define an accepted set of works – books, paintings, etc. – as intrinsically valuable. Usually seen as elitist. Postmodernists strongly attack the distinction between High and Low Culture because it implies the possibility of accurate value judgments.

Hyper-choice
The explosion of different life choices in all areas in this generation. Hyper-choice frequently hinders the act of choosing because we are presented with too many options.

Hyper-reality
The idea that we have no access to the world that is not mediated to us by others, especially the media. Hence we are unable to speak of reality because we are unsure whether what we perceive is real or mediated. Hyper-reality is a key phrase in the work of Jean Baudrillard.

Intention
The desire of a writer or speaker to communicate a particular meaning. Postmodernists deny this is possible. Instead they place decisions about meaning not in the intention of the writer but in the mind of the reader or community of readers.

Legitimation
The process by which we establish the foundations of what we know. Postmodernists say there is currently a crisis of legitimation and that we can only appeal to other knowledge, which itself needs legitimation, *ad infinitum* – i.e. there are no final grounds for knowing anything.

Mass Culture
See 'High Culture' above.

Metanarrative
A big story. Specifically a story that claims to explain all other stories, such as Marxism, Islam or Christianity. Postmodernists say that this is simply a means of imposing power on others, and therefore is unethical.

Micronarrative
It is now suggested that if metanarratives are obsolete, then what is important is the small story of individuals and groups, often those thought to have been oppressed by metanarratives. These small stories are called micronarratives.

Modernism
Generally used to mean the period when scientific progress was seen as the ultimate answer to human need. Measurement was believed to be the way to understand reality, and religion was strongly attacked as anti-rational. The period is hard to date accurately, and in some senses is still with us. It found its high-

est expression in the Industrial Revolution and the French Revolution which practically enshrined Reason as a god.

New Age religion
A pick-and-mix approach to belief. Rather than opting for one coherent set of beliefs, New Age adopts a relativist approach. It is okay to take attractive elements from a variety of sources in order to construct a world-view. These sources do not have to be coherent, because what matters is not whether they are right, but whether they seem useful, usually for self-empowerment.

Nomadism
The idea that the knowing subject (i.e. the 'I' who knows things) is not static, but somehow roams. Linked to the idea that the mind and the person are a bit like a desert – you know it is there, but as the edges of the sand/persona shift, we cannot really tell quite what makes up the person.

Objective
The idea that things can be really known truly. Objectiveness implies a position from outside from which to observe. Postmodernists believe there is no such position. Christians believe that God has such a position and reveals from it.

Pluralism
comes in two forms. Social pluralism is okay – it simply means we live in a multi-faceted, multi-cultural society. Philosophical pluralism, on the other hand, is dangerous. It is the idea that if all truth is relative (see 'Relativism' below), then all ideas and truth claims are equally valid. Under this sort of pluralism anyone who says there are more grounds for their truth claim than someone else's is being an oppressor.

Popular Culture
See 'High Culture' above.

Post-colonialism
The branch of Postmodernism that deals with society in the aftermath of colonialism.

Postmodernism
is a philosophical position based on Postmodernity. When Postmodernity starts to deliberately support itself by developing a theory, then Postmodernism has arrived. Hence the word describes both a culture and a theory, each with a vested interest in maintaining the other.

Postmodernity
The various cultural, technological and sociological factors that have made up mainly capitalist cultures from the middle of the twentieth century.

Post-structuralism
See 'Structuralism' below. Post-structuralism is closely connected to Postmodernism. As Postmodernism refutes the conclusions of Modernism that science provides meaning, so Post-structuralism refutes the idea that meaning can be discovered by analysing ideas and thoughts. Post-structuralism says that ideas and thoughts are not available to analyse structurally, and hence it dismisses meaning altogether.

Pragmatism
A philosophy that judges something according to how useful it is to a group or individual. 'Does it work?' is the question asked by pragmatism. In some senses it is a good question – if something is true it ought to work – but Postmodernists use pragmatism as the only test of value. If an object, idea or person has no inherent value, then the only thing that provides worth is whether it seems useful.

Reflexivity
Reflexivity describes what happens when something turns in on itself. Postmodernism is a self-reflexive phenomenon – it is a theory that produces a culture that itself has the aim of upholding the theory.

Relativism
The idea that nothing is valued by comparison to an absolute standard. Thus all objects, people and truth claims only relate to each other, and can only be said to have relative value or meaning.

Semiotics
The study of signs. Earlier in the century it was thought that all communication could be reduced to signs that could then be perfectly analysed. Postmodernists fiercely disagree with this, suggesting that there is no intrinsic connection between a sign and what it signifies. For example, the word 'dog' has no necessary connection to the animal – it is just a word. However, the Postmodernists go further to suggest that because there is no intrinsic connection, therefore there is no connection at all – and words can never really communicate for this reason.

Simulation
The idea that a replica can replace an original. In the work of Baudrillard we find the idea that the whole world has been replaced by a simulation of itself – so that we can never really know reality.

Structuralism
The idea that meaning is obtainable by reducing ideas and thoughts to their basic structures which can then be analysed. This was very important in the study of linguistics in the early twentieth century. Structuralism suggests that meaning is perfectly definable.

Subjective
The idea that the perception of the individual is the closest we may get to knowing truth. Hence something can be true for one person and not true for someone else. See also 'Objective' above.

Tolerance
A big buzz word, usually taken to mean 'let anything go'. Christians badly need to reclaim the proper meaning of this word – allowing other points of view without having to agree and with all parties being open to discuss and disagree.

Truth
That which corresponds to reality. Christians know that God holds truth, that he reveals things truly and that the revelation can be known. Postmodernists don't think truth exists.

Value
The respective importance we attach to things, ideas and people. Postmodernists hold that all values can only be relative to each other and that there is nothing that is absolutely valuable. Christians hold that some things are absolutely valuable because God has revealed this to be so, and other things are personal preference.

Appendix 2
Suggestions for Further Reading

Here are some suggestions for further reading. The list is far from exhaustive but offers material that I have found helpful and thought-provoking when preparing this book.

Essays quoted in *Meltdown*

Unfortunately for copyright reasons it isn't possible to include the essays discussed in this guide. This is only a very cursory list intended to get you going. There is lots more good secular material available but comparatively little in the way of good Christian response so far. All these essays are hard to read but vital for Christians to understand and engage with.

Michel Foucault, 'What Is An Author?' in *The Foucault Reader* (New York: Random House, 1984), ed. Paul Rabinow.

Jacques Derrida, 'Structure, Sign and Play In the Discourse of the Human Sciences' in *The Structuralist Controversy: The Languages of Criticism and the Sciences of Man* (Baltimore, 1972).

Walter Benjamin, 'The Work of Art in the Age of Its Mechanical Reproduction' in *Illuminations* (London: Jonathan Cape, 1970).

Judith Butler, 'Subjects of Sex/Gender/Desire' in *Gender Trouble – Feminism And The Subversion Of Identity* (Routledge, 1989).

Jean Baudrillard, 'The Precession of Simulacra' in *Simulations* (New York: Semiotextée, 1983).

Easy books that include sections that relate to Postmodernism – useful for an overview

Postmodernism For Beginners by Richard Appignanesi and Chris Garratt (Icon Books). Not a Christian book, but incisive and witty. A history of contemporary ideas in cartoons!

Blind Alley Beliefs by David Cook (IVP). The popular radio figure takes a close look at the ideological 'isms' of our day and shows how each makes claims about the meaning of human life. The book tests each alternative against Christianity by asking three questions: 'Is the belief self-consistent?', 'Does it correspond to the known facts?' and 'Does it work?'

Facing the Challenge of Our Times by David Couchman (Focus Christian Radio). Not so much a book as a course to help you be confident in the truth of the good news. Insightful comment, discussion questions, home assignments – excellent for either group or personal use.

Alt.Culture by Steven Daly and Nathaniel Wice (HarperPerennial). A mid-ninties A to Z of culture. From *Absolutely Fabulous* to Frank Zappa, *Baywatch* to Warhol, an eclectic guide to culture 'underground, online and over the counter'.

The Invasion of the Computer Culture by Allen Emerson and Cheryl Forbes (IVP). An easy-to-read account of the transforming effect of new technology on society and on ourselves, with a clear call to let our thinking be shaped not by our technology but by our God.

The Gravedigger File (Hodder and Stoughton) and *Time For Truth* (IVP) by Os Guiness. *The Gravedigger File* is an entertaining and thoughtful romp through the large-scale influences on culture and the church over recent years. Presented in the manner of C. S. Lewis' *The Screwtape Letters*, a defector changes sides, bringing secret papers on the subversion of the modern church. Fun to read as well as perceptive. *Time for Truth* is a book on 'living free in a world of lies, hype and spin'. It's all about integrity and the fact that genuine freedom depends on there being truth at the heart of the universe. Lots of contemporary illustrations.

Transmission (IVP) and *Truth – Could It Be True?* (Solway) by Peter Hicks. *Transmission* deals entertainingly with questions about belief in a Postmodern age from a student to a Christian. It circles these key questions around with stories, anecdotes and plenty of stimulating material presented in refreshing and challenging ways for a new generation. Excellent both for content and method. *Truth – Could It Be True?* advertises itself as a non-frightening book about philosophy. It succeeds in presenting issues of the knowability of objective truth in easy-to-grasp, inviting ways.

Evangelism Made Slightly Less Difficult by Nick Pollard (IVP). An easy-to-read and stimulating book on evangelism that is particularly good on understanding the contemporary world-views of those we are trying to tell about Jesus.

The Universe Next Door, Discipleship of the Mind, Why Should Anyone Believe Anything At All?, The Universe Upstairs (cartoons!) by James Sire (all in IVP). Nobody does popular books on thinking and culture like James Sire. All highly recommended, especially *Discipleship of the Mind*, which asks the crucial question, 'How can we learn to love God in the ways that we think?' Also full of suggestions on approaching academic study as a Christian.

A Guide to Contemporary Culture by Gene Veith (IVP). A wide-ranging but easy survey of Western society as a whole, the beliefs that underlie it and where it is heading.

Medium-difficulty books that include sections that relate to Postmodernism – useful for more depth.

The Discerning Reader by David Barratt, Roger Pooley and Leyland Ryken (Apollos). An excellent Christian response for those studying literature, including sample essay material as well as discerning comment on Christian approaches to literature.

The Idea of the Postmodern by Hans Bertens (Routledge). A good secular reader.

Postmodernist Culture and *Theory and Cultural Value* by Stephen Connor (Blackwells). *Postmodernist Culture* is probably the best secular introduction to the field of contemporary culture and theory. Connor reflects on a large number of disciplines and institutions including TV, video and film. *Theory and Cultural Value* is a harder read but provides a stimulating survey of the way that different disciplines ascribe value to things in culture – psychoanalysis, Marxism, feminism, Postmodernism etc.

The best medium-weight books on living as God's people in today's culture

Truth Decay by Douglas Groothuis (IVP). A great Christian book on truth and culture that treads the tightrope between being too deep and too shallow without falling off! It deals well with secular authors, has the best chapters I have yet read on Christianity and art and ethics in a Postmodern world, and has a chapter on television designed to challenge and provoke. Highly recommended.

Virtual Morality by Graham Houston (IVP). This book asks the question, 'How does a Christian ethic speak to new technology and technological change?' It deals with the phenomenon of simulation, the place of ethics in a world dominated by virtuality, and the public nature of Christian truth, among other things.

Issues Facing Christians Today, *More Issues Facing Christians Today* (both HarperCollins) and *The Contemporary Christian* by John Stott (IVP). John Stott's insightful writings on living as a Christian in a morally complex modern world need no commendation. They should be required reading for all Christians.

No Place for Truth, *God in the Wasteland* and *Losing Our Virtue* by David Wells (all in IVP). *No Place for Truth* traces and analyses the decline in evangelical theology and the state of evangelical belief in truth in the modern West. *God in the Wasteland*, subtitled *The Reality of Truth in a World of Fading Dreams*, asks what effect the church might have on the culture when we pour ourselves out in costly service and proclaim the weighty glory of God. *Losing Our Virtue – Why the Church Must Recover Its Moral Vision* is, in my view, the best of the three books. It examines the effect of a relativist world-view on self, society, church and belief, concluding that the result is loss of confidence in the eternal Word of God that must be recovered, or we will die.

Harder books – don't say you weren't warned!

The books listed below (apart from Lyotard) are Christian responses to various areas of theory.

The Gagging of God by Don Carson (Apollos). Helpful, if daunting, treatment of the confrontation between Christianity and pluralism. Carson makes the vital contribution of putting lots of secular pace-setting theorists before his readers with insightful and discerning critique. The first half, on the general phenomenon of pluralism, is competent; the second, on Christian pluralism and evangelical fragmentation, is superb.

The Postmodern Condition by Jean-Francois Lyotard (Manchester University Press). The seminal, if confused, book on thinking that made so much Postmodern thought concrete. Originally a treatise on the state of knowledge prepared for the French government, *The Postmodern Condition* has revolutionized all academic study and secular teaching about thought. All secular writing of the last twenty years about discourse, interpretation, thinking and truth recognizes its debt to Lyotard's book. Short and tricky but worth persevering with if you are keen to know exactly where a lot of today's ideas have come from.

The Recovery of Mission by Vinoth Ramachandra (Paternoster). For those interested in the effects of multi-cultural society on ideas about truth, this excellent book takes three influential Asian pluralists and argues for the decisive uniqueness of Jesus, regardless of our cultural heritage.

Modern Art and the Death of a Culture by H. R. Rookmaaker (Apollos). Now slightly dated but never bettered, Rookmaaker traces how so many of the movements in today's culture are connected with despair and nihilism in the art world. For those wanting a grip on the world of modern art, where so many cultural phenomena begin, this is a good place to start.

A Christian View of Philosophy and Culture and *A Christian View of the West* by Francis Schaeffer (both in Crossway). Volumes 1 and 5 of Schaeffer's *Complete Works* remain one of the most influential Christian treatments of the subject.

Is There a Meaning in this Text? by Kevin Vanhoozer (Apollos). Deals superbly with the whole question of whether meaning is accessible through a text. Probably the best Christian treatment of the subject. Hard reading.

Websites

Marcus Honeysett's personal site
www.mhoneysett.freeserve.co.uk
Contains additional material relevant to *Meltdown*, available for free download

The Damaris Project
www.damaris.org
Perhaps the world's best site examining contemporary culture from a Christian perspective. Thousands of well-organized pages on books, films, plays, ideas and theories. Highly recommended.

Notes

1. Quoted in Vinoth Ramachandra, *The Recovery of Mission* (Paternoster), p. 50.
2. Wayne Grudem, *Systematic Theology* (IVP), p. 49.
3. David Wells, *God in the Wasteland* (IVP), p. 121.
4. David Wells, *Losing Our Virtue* (IVP), p. 44.
5. Ibid., p. 120.
6. Ibid., pp. 62–63.
7. Douglas Groothuis, *Truth Decay* (IVP), p. 282.
8. H. R. Rookmaaker, *Modern Art and the Death of a Culture* (Apollos), p. 200.
9. Groothuis, *Truth Decay*, p. 284.
10. Wells, *Losing Our Virtue*, p. 26.